Graboids and Garland

Graboids and Garland

Matthew Petchinsky

Graboids and Garland: The Ultimate Tremors-Themed Christmas Guide

By: Matthew Petchinsky

Disclaimer:
This is an independent, fan-created work inspired by the *Tremors* film series. It is not affil-
iated with, endorsed by, or connected to Universal Pictures, Stampede Entertainment, or
any other rights holders of the *Tremors* franchise. All trademarks, characters, and related
elements of *Tremors* remain the property of their respective owners. This book is intended
for entertainment and educational purposes only and draws on publicly available informa-
tion and original creative content.

Welcome to the Tremors Wonderland

The holidays are here, and it's time to deck the halls—but with a monstrous twist. If you're tired of the same old Christmas tropes and looking for something that blends festive cheer with thrilling chaos, you've found your perfect holiday companion. Welcome to **Tremors Wonderland**, where we transform the season of joy into a Graboid-infested celebration of epic proportions.

This guide is for those who dare to take Christmas off the beaten path. It's for movie buffs who appreciate the comedic terror of the *Tremors* franchise and for holiday rebels who want a theme that's as fun as it is fearsome. Whether you're a long-time fan of the cult-classic series or just discovering the thrill of battling subterranean monsters, this fusion of horror-comedy and seasonal spirit is guaranteed to inject excitement into your winter festivities.

Why *Tremors*?

The *Tremors* movies, which started with the 1990 cult masterpiece starring Kevin Bacon, introduced us to the terrifying yet oddly charming Graboids—massive, carnivorous creatures that tunnel beneath the earth and strike when you least expect it. What sets the franchise apart is its perfect mix of humor, horror, and heart. It's not just a monster movie; it's a rollercoaster of survival, wit, and camaraderie.

Now imagine that vibe woven into the fabric of your holiday season. The winter months may be cold and quiet, but in Tremors Wonderland, the ground is always shaking with excitement. From **Graboid-themed decorations** and **creature-inspired treats** to the ultimate *Tremors* movie marathon, we'll show you how to turn your home into a monster-loving festive haven that'll have your friends and family talking for years.

A Wonderland of Creativity

Creating a Tremors-inspired Christmas is all about creativity, humor, and a little DIY ingenuity. Here's what you can expect in this guide:

- **Graboids in the Décor**: Step aside, elves and reindeer—this year's centerpiece is a *Graboid*. We'll cover how to craft unique decorations, from monstrous stockings to a "bursting out of the floor" Graboid prop.
- **Festive Fear Foods**: Move over gingerbread men. It's time for *Graboid cupcakes*, "worm-tunnel spaghetti," and more monstrously delicious treats to fuel your Tremors celebrations.
- **Tremors Movie Marathon**: Whether you're starting from the original *Tremors* or diving into all seven films, we've mapped out the ultimate movie marathon experience. Complete with themed snacks, drinks, and viewing-party ideas.
- **Games and Activities**: Keep the fun going with Tremors trivia, Graboid scavenger hunts, and Christmas horror games that bring the monster mayhem to life.

For the Horror-Comedy Fanatics

Horror-comedy holds a special place in pop culture. It's the genre that doesn't take itself too seriously while delivering all the chills and thrills we crave. The *Tremors* franchise epitomizes that balance—it keeps us on edge while letting us laugh along with its quirky characters and over-the-top action. A Tremors Christmas is the perfect way to celebrate this unique genre and give the holiday season a much-needed jolt of adrenaline.

If you're someone who loves unconventional holidays, laughs in the face of fear, and enjoys turning tradition on its head, then you've come to the right place. This guide is your ticket to a holiday season that's equal parts cozy and chaotic, with just the right amount of monster madness to keep things unforgettable.

So grab your Santa hat and your survival gear—it's time to bring the Graboids home for the holidays. Welcome to the *Tremors Wonderland*. Let's make this Christmas one for the ages, where the ground shakes with festive cheer and the monsters are the guests of honor.

Happy Holidays and **Beware the Graboids!** ◈◈

Part 1: Tremors-Themed Decorations

Chapter 1: Crafting Graboid Garlands and Ornaments

Welcome to the heart of your *Tremors* Wonderland transformation! A Christmas tree adorned with glittering stars, cozy garlands, and candy canes is a classic sight—but what if you could add some monstrous *Tremors* flair? In this chapter, we'll dive into the world of DIY holiday décor with Graboid garlands, ornaments, and other festive monster-inspired crafts. By the end, your home will boast unique decorations that celebrate both the spirit of the season and the subterranean horrors of Perfection Valley.

1.1 Graboid Garland: The Perfect Festive Touch

A *Graboid Garland* is a fun and easy way to infuse your holiday space with underground monster vibes. These garlands feature stringed "Graboids" tunneling their way across your mantel, tree, or windows. The best part? They're customizable, easy to make with common craft supplies, and guaranteed to spark conversation.

Supplies You'll Need

- Brown, black, and beige construction paper or felt (for Graboid bodies)
- Twine, string, or holiday garland base
- Googly eyes or craft foam (for monster details)
- Hot glue gun or craft glue
- Scissors
- Markers or paint (optional for detail work)
- Mini bells or red bows (for festive accents)

Step-by-Step Guide to Crafting the Garland

1. **Cut Out Your Graboids**
   - Start by cutting out Graboid shapes from brown construction paper or felt. Think worm-like, elongated bodies with slightly jagged edges for an organic, monstrous feel. Each Graboid should be about 4–6 inches long.
   - Cut small triangle pieces for the "mouths" and use black or red construction paper to add teeth or tongues. For added detail, consider layering beige paper for a sand-like effect.

2. **Add Monster Features**
   - Glue googly eyes or small black foam circles onto the body of each Graboid. If you want to mimic the *Tremors* creature more closely, draw or cut "tentacles" peeking out of the mouths.

- Use black markers or paint to create shading, ridges, and lines across the body for texture.

3. **Assemble the Garland**
   - Cut a piece of twine or string to your desired length. Space the Graboids about 6 inches apart along the twine, gluing them in place. Make sure the "mouths" of the Graboids face outward for maximum monster appeal.
   - Attach festive touches like small bells, miniature bows, or glitter to add a hint of Christmas cheer while keeping with the Tremors theme.

4. **Hang and Enjoy**
   - Drape your Graboid garland on the Christmas tree, across the mantel, or along doorways. The sight of monstrous worms wiggling their way through your holiday décor is sure to bring smiles and shivers.

1.2 Graboid Tree Ornaments: Worms on the Tree

What's a *Tremors Wonderland* without a Christmas tree covered in "underground" terror? Crafting Graboid ornaments is not only easy but also a great activity to involve kids, family, or friends in the festive fun.

Supplies You'll Need

- Polymer clay or air-dry clay (brown, black, and beige)
- Craft paint (red, black, white)
- String or ornament hooks
- Small paintbrushes
- Optional: Glitter or fake snow spray for added flair

Step-by-Step Instructions for Graboid Ornaments

1. **Shape the Graboids**
   - Take a ball of brown polymer clay or air-dry clay and roll it into a worm-like shape (about 3–4 inches long). Add slight bends and curves to make the "Graboid" look like it's in motion.
   - Sculpt the mouth by creating a wide opening on one end and shaping small "tentacle" appendages inside. Add jagged teeth by pressing small white clay pieces into the mouth opening.
2. **Bake or Dry**
   - If using polymer clay, follow the instructions on the package for baking the ornaments. If air-dry clay is your choice, let the pieces dry completely overnight.
3. **Paint the Details**
   - Use black paint to add ridges or texture lines across the worm's body. Paint the teeth white, and use red paint to add a gory tongue or accents inside the mouth. For a final touch, add black "sand-like" shading along the edges for an underground feel.
   - If you're feeling festive, sprinkle glitter or fake snow spray for a wintry Graboid effect.
4. **Add Hanging Loops**
   - Attach string or ornament hooks by either gluing them into the top of the Graboid or carefully piercing a hole at the top of the ornament before baking/drying.
5. **Hang the Graboids**
   - Place the Graboids on your Christmas tree, spacing them among lights, ribbons, and baubles. The terrifying sight of these worms "emerging" from the branches will make your tree a showstopper.

1.3 Bonus Monster-Inspired Crafts

If you're ready to take the Tremors theme even further, here are a few quick and creative ideas for additional crafts:

- **Graboid Stockings**: Use brown felt or fabric to create custom Christmas stockings that look like a Graboid's open mouth. Add jagged teeth around the opening and hang them on the mantel.
- **Sand Trap Snow Globes**: Fill clear mason jars or glass globes with sand, small toy worms (or mini clay Graboids), and faux snow. Shake it up for a wintry "Tremors" snow globe.
- **Perfection Valley Wreath**: Create a holiday wreath using twigs, sand-colored burlap ribbon, and small Graboid crafts glued around it. Add a festive "Welcome to Perfection" sign in the center.

Conclusion: A DIY Wonderland of Monsters

Crafting *Tremors*-themed garlands, ornaments, and monster-inspired décor is an exciting way to blend your love of horror-comedy with holiday cheer. These unique, handmade decorations don't just make for great conversation starters—they also celebrate the creativity and humor that make *Tremors* a cult classic.

With Graboids tunneling across your mantel and worm-like horrors perched on your tree, your home will transform into a *Tremors Wonderland* like no other. Let your inner artist run wild, involve your family or friends, and enjoy the process of creating holiday décor that's equal parts creepy and festive.

Chapter 2: The "Seismic Tree" Setup

The Christmas tree is the centerpiece of any holiday celebration, but in *Tremors Wonderland*, it becomes a thrilling masterpiece that combines festive charm with underground monster madness. Forget the usual glittering stars and angel toppers—this year's tree will quake with seismic flair, showcasing Graboids, desert aesthetics, and an unexpected explosion of creative details.

In this chapter, you'll learn how to craft and decorate a **"Seismic Tree"** that would look right at home in Perfection Valley. From selecting the perfect color schemes and lighting setups to designing one-of-a-kind toppers and ornaments, we'll guide you step by step to create a tree that's equal parts Christmas cheer and *Tremors* chaos.

2.1 Designing the Seismic Theme

Before diving into the setup, it's important to decide on the overall look and feel of your "Seismic Tree." The goal is to capture the essence of the *Tremors* world—rugged, dusty desert landscapes mixed with hints of monster terror—while keeping it festive and visually stunning.

Color Scheme

- **Earthy Tones**: Start with a palette inspired by the desert. Think **sandy browns, deep oranges, beige, and muted yellows** to represent the arid ground where Graboids thrive.
- **Accents of Red and Black**: Use **black** for the shadowy tunnels and **red** to represent Graboid mouths or seismic warnings. These bold colors will give your tree a dramatic and thrilling pop.
- **Metallic Gold or Silver**: A few metallic touches will keep the tree festive while maintaining the rugged theme. Use gold for highlights that mimic sunlight hitting the desert surface.

Tree Type and Setup

- Opt for a natural-looking artificial tree or a real tree with a fuller shape, as its rugged greenery will serve as the perfect "terrain" for the decorations.
- If you're feeling bold, lightly dust the tree with **brown spray paint or faux sand spray** (optional) to give it a desert-like texture. Alternatively, use burlap ribbons or sand-colored garlands to weave through the branches for an "earthy" look.

2.2 Lights: The Tremors Glow

No tree is complete without a brilliant light display, but for the Seismic Tree, the lighting needs to channel a sense of underground danger and seismic energy. Here's how to light it up:

Choosing Lights

- **Warm White or Amber Lights**: Use warm white LED lights to create a soft desert glow reminiscent of sunlight over Perfection Valley. This keeps the base of your tree warm and inviting.
- **Red Accent Lights**: Strategically weave in red LED lights to give the tree an ominous, "seismic warning" effect. Use these sparingly to highlight key areas, like the base of the tree where Graboids "emerge."
- **Flickering Lights**: For added drama, incorporate flickering lights or string lights with a "firelight" effect to simulate the ground shaking and energy bursting through the earth.

Placement Tips

- Start with the warm white lights as a base, wrapping them evenly from the center out toward the tips of the branches.
- Layer the red accent lights closer to the trunk or bottom of the tree to mimic seismic activity happening "underground."
- Tuck flickering lights randomly within the branches to create a sense of movement and chaos—perfect for a *Tremors* theme!

2.3 Seismic Tree Toppers: A Graboid Finale

The topper is where your creativity can truly shine. Instead of a traditional angel or star, let's bring a **Graboid** to life at the peak of your tree. Here are three monstrous options:

Option 1: DIY Graboid Bursting Through

- Craft a Graboid head using **foam or air-dry clay**. Shape the mouth open wide, with jagged teeth and tongue details painted red and white.
- Attach tentacle-like "snakes" emerging from the mouth using twisted brown construction paper or felt.
- Mount the Graboid head at the top of the tree so it looks like it's bursting out of the branches, mouth open and ready to strike.

Option 2: "Seismic Star"

- Create a custom star topper that mimics seismic activity. Use a cardboard base, painted **black with red cracks** to look like fissures in the earth.
- Add LED lights or red glitter accents to make it glow ominously at the top of the tree.
- Optional: Glue small clay Graboids or mini desert props onto the star for added detail.

Option 3: Tremors Warning Sign

- Print or hand-paint a sign that reads **"CAUTION: SEISMIC ACTIVITY—BEWARE OF GRABOIDS"** on a wooden or foam board. Use distressed lettering and weathering effects to make it look authentic.
- Attach it as a playful and attention-grabbing topper that reinforces your *Tremors* theme.

2.4 Ornaments and Finishing Touches

Your Seismic Tree needs to tell a story, and each ornament is a chance to add detail and personality to its underground monster vibe.

DIY Graboid Ornaments

As described in Chapter 1, craft Graboid ornaments using polymer clay or felt, and hang them throughout the tree. Position them to look like they're "tunneling" through the branches.

Desert Terrain Accents

- Use small burlap bags or pouches filled with faux sand or pebbles as tree ornaments. Add tiny labels like "Perfection Valley Soil" for a quirky touch.
- Scatter twigs, faux cacti, or dried flowers throughout the branches to simulate desert plants.

Seismic Warning Props

- Print mini "SEISMIC WARNING" signs on cardstock, weather them with brown paint or tea stains, and hang them like ornaments.
- Cut jagged "cracks" out of black construction paper and attach them to branches to mimic fissures caused by underground activity.

Final Festive Touches

- Add touches of fake snow sparingly to contrast with the earthy tones and create a "desert-in-winter" aesthetic.
- Tie burlap ribbons or twine bows for a rugged finish, and scatter small pinecones or rocks at the tree's base for a realistic desert vibe.

2.5 Displaying Your Seismic Tree

The tree is ready to make its grand debut, but its setting is just as important. Enhance the Seismic Tree's impact with a themed **tree skirt** and surrounding décor:

- **Tree Skirt**: Use burlap fabric, sand-colored felt, or printed material that looks like cracked earth or desert terrain. Scatter small Graboid props or toy worms near the base.
- **Surrounding Décor**: Place faux rocks, wooden crates, and a few "seismic warning" signs around the tree. For added flair, include a toy truck or miniature DIY town sign that reads "Welcome to Perfection."

Conclusion: The Centerpiece of Your Wonderland

Your Seismic Tree is now ready to steal the show—a monstrous masterpiece that perfectly blends Christmas magic with *Tremors* thrills. Whether it's the glowing red accents, the carefully crafted Graboid topper, or the rugged desert aesthetic, your tree will become the centerpiece of a *Tremors Wonderland* like no other.

Chapter 3: Graboid Stockings for the Fireplace

No Christmas setup is complete without stockings hanging by the fireplace, ready to be stuffed with gifts and treats. But in *Tremors Wonderland*, stockings aren't just simple fabric pouches—they become monstrous masterpieces inspired by Graboids. In this chapter, we'll explore how to create or customize **Graboid Stockings** that are both festive and terrifying. Whether you're an experienced sewer, a DIY beginner, or someone looking to purchase unique stockings, this guide has you covered.

3.1 Designing Your Graboid Stockings

Before diving into the sewing or crafting process, it's essential to conceptualize what your Graboid-inspired stocking will look like. The stockings can range from subtle hints of monster madness to full-blown replicas of a Graboid mouth ready to "chomp" on Christmas treats.

Design Ideas

1. **Graboid Mouth Stocking**
   - This design makes the stocking look like the gaping mouth of a Graboid. Jagged teeth form the top edge, while the "tongue" of the stocking hangs down to hold gifts.
2. **Graboid Skin Stocking**
   - Use fabric or paint to replicate the earthy, rugged texture of Graboid skin, complete with ridges and shadowing. Add "tentacles" or worm-like appendages for an extra touch.
3. **Seismic Warning Stocking**
   - Combine festive and horror themes with a stocking that mimics a seismic warning sign. Use phrases like "Caution: Graboid Territory" or "Beware of Tunneling Worms" for an eye-catching design.

3.2 Materials Needed

Here's a list of supplies to get you started, whether you're sewing your stocking from scratch or customizing pre-made ones:

For Sewing from Scratch

- **Fabric**:
    - Brown felt, burlap, or faux suede for a rugged "Graboid skin" look.
    - Black, red, or white felt for the mouth, teeth, and tongue details.
- **Thread**: Thick, sturdy thread in matching colors.
- **Scissors**: Fabric scissors for precision cuts.
- **Sewing Machine or Needle**: Depending on whether you prefer hand-sewing or machine sewing.
- **Hot Glue Gun**: For attaching embellishments like teeth and tentacles.
- **Stuffing Material** (optional): Cotton or polyester filling to give the stocking structure.
- **Ribbon or Twine**: For hanging the stockings.

For Customizing Pre-Made Stockings

- Plain stockings (red, brown, or beige work best as a base).
- Felt or foam sheets for crafting Graboid features (teeth, tentacles, tongues).
- Fabric paint in earthy tones (brown, black, beige, and red).
- Hot glue gun or fabric glue.
- Googly eyes, small bells, or other accents for extra flair.

3.3 Sewing Your Own Graboid Stocking
Step 1: Cutting Out the Fabric

1. **Trace and Cut the Stocking Shape**
   - Draw a stocking template on paper or cardboard. Use a traditional stocking shape but allow extra space at the top for the Graboid mouth.
   - Cut two identical stocking shapes from brown or burlap fabric.
2. **Prepare the Graboid Mouth**
   - Cut a jagged "mouth" edge for one of the stocking pieces. This will serve as the top opening. Use red felt for the interior of the mouth and white felt for the teeth.
   - Optional: Cut a long red "tongue" to hang inside the stocking.

Step 2: Assembling the Stocking

1. **Attach the Mouth Details**
   - Sew or glue the red felt (mouth interior) to the jagged top edge of one stocking piece.
   - Glue the white felt "teeth" along the edge of the red felt, overlapping slightly.
   - If adding a tongue, attach it to the inside of the stocking near the mouth opening.
2. **Sew the Stocking Together**
   - Place the two stocking pieces together, right sides facing inward. Sew around the edges, leaving the top open.
   - Turn the stocking right-side out and press it flat.
3. **Add Graboid Texture and Features**
   - Use black fabric paint or a marker to draw ridges, lines, and spots for texture. You can also glue small pieces of brown felt to create raised "skin folds."
   - Optional: Sew or glue "tentacles" made of twisted felt or fabric strips onto the sides of the stocking.
4. **Finish with a Hanging Loop**
   - Attach a ribbon or twine loop to the top corner of the stocking for easy hanging.

3.4 Customizing Pre-Made Stockings

If sewing isn't your thing, don't worry—you can transform plain store-bought stockings into Graboid-themed creations in just a few steps.

Step-by-Step Instructions

1. **Create the Graboid Mouth**
   - Cut jagged teeth from white felt and a mouth interior from red felt. Glue these to the top edge of the stocking to mimic a Graboid's open mouth.
2. **Add Texture and Details**
   - Use brown and black fabric paint to create the rough, worm-like texture of a Graboid. Add ridges, dirt spots, and shading for a realistic effect.
   - Attach googly eyes or felt "tentacles" to make the stocking more monstrous.
3. **Personalize with Seismic Warnings**
   - Paint or glue small signs onto the stocking that say "Beware of Graboids" or "Seismic Activity Detected." These little touches add humor and reinforce the theme.
4. **Festive Accents**
   - Attach small bells, twine bows, or burlap trim to balance the rugged Graboid aesthetic with a bit of Christmas charm.

3.5 Where to Purchase Graboid-Inspired Stockings

If you'd prefer to purchase pre-made Graboid stockings, consider these options:

- **Custom Crafters**: Search for artists on Etsy or other handmade marketplaces who offer custom monster stockings. Provide them with your *Tremors*-inspired ideas for a one-of-a-kind creation.
- **DIY Shops**: Stores like Michaels or Hobby Lobby sell plain stockings and Graboid-appropriate craft supplies that make quick customization easy.
- **Online Retailers**: While you may not find *official* Graboid stockings, monster-themed stockings are readily available. Look for "monster mouth" or "creature-inspired" designs that you can tweak to fit the theme.

3.6 Stuffing the Stockings: Graboid Goodies

Once your Graboid stockings are ready to hang, it's time to fill them with themed goodies that match your *Tremors Wonderland*. Here are some ideas:

- **Mini Graboid Figures**: Small worm-like toys or collectibles.
- **Seismic Candy**: Earthquake-themed chocolates, gummy worms, or dirt cake mixes.
- ***Tremors* Merchandise**: DVDs, shirts, or keychains from the *Tremors* franchise.
- **Tools for Survival**: Flashlights, mini shovels, or emergency whistles—playful nods to surviving Graboid attacks.
- **Monster-Inspired Snacks**: Packets of popcorn (perfect for a *Tremors* movie night).

Conclusion: A Monstrous Fireplace Setup

With Graboid stockings hanging ominously by the fireplace, your *Tremors Wonderland* is one step closer to completion. These monstrous stockings are sure to thrill horror fans, spark conversation, and make for an unforgettable holiday tradition. Whether you sew your own masterpiece or customize pre-made ones, your attention to detail will bring the underground terror of Graboids to life.

Chapter 4: Creating a Tremors-Inspired Wreath

Nothing says "Welcome to *Tremors Wonderland*" like a front door that hints at the subterranean chaos lurking beneath your holiday décor. The wreath—typically a festive, cheerful decoration—is getting a monstrous makeover. In this chapter, we'll guide you step-by-step to build a **Tremors-Inspired Wreath** featuring desert sand textures, wriggling Graboid tentacles, and just the right amount of festive flair to keep it holiday-appropriate. Whether you hang it on your front door, over your fireplace, or in your living room, this wreath will serve as a chilling yet playful homage to the Graboids of *Perfection Valley*.

4.1 The Concept: A Blend of Terror and Holiday Cheer

The *Tremors*-inspired wreath combines the eerie desert aesthetic of the franchise with traditional Christmas wreath elements. Picture this: a rugged, earthy base with Graboids' tentacles bursting out, dusted with faux sand and accented by small hints of red and green to maintain a holiday touch.

The result? A wreath that says **"Welcome to Perfection Valley—if you dare!"**

4.2 Materials Needed

To bring your monstrous wreath to life, gather the following supplies:

For the Base

- A plain wreath base (grapevine wreath, foam wreath, or wire wreath frame)
- Burlap ribbon or sand-colored fabric for wrapping
- Faux moss, twigs, and dried grass for desert texture
- Craft glue or hot glue gun

For the Tentacles

- Brown or beige pool noodles (for larger tentacles)
- Brown felt, fabric, or clay (for smaller tentacle details)
- Red or black craft paint (for accents and details)
- Scissors and craft knife

For Sand and Details

- Fine craft sand (tan or light brown)
- Clear spray adhesive (to help sand stick)
- Optional: Small rocks, pebbles, or desert plant accents (mini succulents or cacti)

For Festive Touches

- Twine or burlap bows
- Small red bells or ornaments
- Mini LED lights (warm white or red)

- Pinecones or faux holly leaves for added texture

4.3 Step-by-Step Instructions for Building the Wreath
Step 1: Wrap the Wreath Base

1. Begin with a plain wreath base such as a grapevine or foam wreath.
2. Wrap the entire base with burlap ribbon or sand-colored fabric. Secure the material with hot glue to create a textured, desert-like appearance.
3. For added ruggedness, glue on small patches of faux moss, dried grass, or twigs. This creates the illusion of dry, cracked terrain where Graboids lurk.

Step 2: Craft the Tentacles
The tentacles are the star of your wreath and will make it unmistakably *Tremors*-themed.

1. **Shaping the Tentacles**:
   - Use pool noodles for larger tentacles. Cut them into varying lengths (6–12 inches) and shape them into curved, worm-like forms. Use a craft knife to trim one end to a point for a tapered look.
   - For smaller tentacles, roll brown felt or clay into elongated shapes and twist them slightly to mimic movement.
2. **Adding Texture**:
   - Paint the pool noodles or felt tentacles in a mix of **brown and beige** to mimic Graboid skin. Add dark shading and subtle red streaks to give the appearance of rugged, earthy texture.
   - Use black paint or marker to create ridges, lines, and dirt smudges for realism.
3. **Attaching Tentacles**:
   - Glue the tentacles at various points around the wreath, positioning them to look as if they're bursting out from the "ground." Angle them in different directions for a dynamic, chaotic appearance.
   - Optional: Wrap one or two tentacles with twine or burlap to give them a festive bow-like effect.

Step 3: Adding the Sand Effect
To truly capture the *Tremors* desert aesthetic, the wreath needs a layer of faux sand.

1. **Spray Adhesive**: Lightly spray sections of the wreath with clear adhesive spray.
2. **Apply Sand**: Sprinkle fine craft sand generously over the glue, focusing on the areas around the tentacles and base. Shake off any excess sand and let it dry completely.
3. **Seal the Sand**: Once the sand has adhered, give the wreath another light coat of adhesive spray to lock the sand in place.

Step 4: Festive Holiday Touches

To blend the monster madness with holiday cheer, add small festive details:

1. **Mini Ornaments and Bells**: Glue small red bells, pinecones, or faux holly leaves between the tentacles. The pop of red contrasts nicely against the brown tones of the wreath.
2. **Burlap or Twine Bow**: Tie a large burlap bow at the bottom or top of the wreath for a rustic holiday finish. If you prefer, attach a red ribbon bow for a bit more color.
3. **LED Lights**: Weave warm white or red LED lights through the wreath for an added glow. Position some lights near the tentacles to create dramatic highlights and shadows.

4.4 Displaying Your Tremors Wreath

Once your wreath is complete, it's time to put it on display. Here are a few suggestions for showcasing your monstrous creation:

1. **Front Door Statement**: Hang the wreath on your front door for maximum impact. Add a "**Caution: Graboids Present**" sign nearby to complete the theme.
2. **Over the Mantel**: Place the wreath above your fireplace or on a prominent wall. Pair it with a Graboid stocking setup (Chapter 3) for a cohesive look.
3. **Dining Room Centerpiece**: Lay the wreath flat on your dining table and place a large red candle or lantern in the center for a stunning and unconventional holiday centerpiece.
4. **Themed Photo Backdrop**: Use the wreath as part of a holiday photo backdrop for parties. It's perfect for guests to take fun, *Tremors*-inspired pictures.

4.5 Maintenance and Storage

To keep your *Tremors*-inspired wreath looking its best:

- **Dust Carefully**: Use a soft brush or compressed air to remove dust from the sand and tentacles.
- **Avoid Moisture**: Store the wreath in a dry location to prevent the sand or paint from deteriorating.
- **Cover for Storage**: Wrap the wreath in plastic or place it in a large box during the off-season to keep it protected.

Conclusion: A Monstrous Welcome to Tremors Wonderland

Your Tremors-inspired wreath is now ready to welcome guests into your festive monster-filled holiday haven. With sand-covered textures, wriggling tentacles, and touches of holiday cheer, this wreath perfectly captures the fun and chaos of a *Tremors Wonderland*. It's a unique statement piece that shows off your creativity and love for this cult-classic franchise while still embracing the spirit of the season.

Chapter 5: Tabletop Terrors: Tremors Table Settings

A proper *Tremors Wonderland* isn't complete without a dinner table that oozes creativity, festive charm, and a touch of subterranean terror. Whether you're hosting a small family gathering, a themed party, or a full-scale *Tremors* movie marathon feast, your table settings should reflect the spirit of Perfection Valley—where dusty deserts meet monstrous surprises. In this chapter, we'll explore step-by-step ideas for creating **Graboid-inspired table settings** with desert aesthetics, clever centerpieces, and thematic place settings to bring your dining experience to life.

5.1 The Theme: Desert Meets Festive Horror

The table design will embrace two main elements: the rugged, earthy aesthetic of the *Tremors* desert setting and holiday-inspired details that tie it all together. The challenge lies in balancing the rustic, wild terrain with subtle festive touches to keep it visually stunning and functional.

Here's what you'll aim to include:

1. **Table Runner**: Sandy tones with cracks, faux rocks, or burlap for texture.
2. **Centerpieces**: Graboids emerging from the "earth" or themed desert decorations.
3. **Place Settings**: Creative plates, name cards, and utensil displays that hint at seismic chaos.
4. **Festive Accents**: A mix of traditional holiday décor and *Tremors*-themed elements like toy trucks, desert plants, or seismic warning signs.

5.2 Table Foundation: Tablecloths and Runners

The base of your table sets the tone for the entire look.

Option 1: Sandy Desert Tablecloth

- Use a **burlap tablecloth** or sand-colored linen to mimic the desert terrain. Burlap works particularly well for adding texture and can be left slightly wrinkled to resemble rugged ground.
- For added flair, use brown or black fabric paint to create cracks or tunnels emerging from random spots on the cloth. Keep the cracks subtle so the table remains functional.

Option 2: DIY Graboid Table Runner

1. **Materials**: Use burlap, kraft paper, or a roll of sand-colored fabric as your table runner.
2. **Cracks and Tunnels**: Draw or paint jagged fissures and cracks along the length of the runner. Add hints of "tentacles" bursting out of these cracks with black or red paint.
3. **Faux Rocks and Sand**: Glue small clusters of faux rocks, pebbles, and moss onto parts of the runner to create a "3D desert" effect. Lightly sprinkle craft sand for an added layer of realism.

5.3 Centerpieces: Graboids on the Table

Your centerpiece is the focal point of the table, and a *Tremors* centerpiece should be a fun, eye-catching homage to the franchise. Here are three creative options:

Option 1: Graboid Bursting Out of the Table

- **Materials**: Foam or clay (for the Graboid), craft sand, faux moss, and twigs.
- **Steps**:
  1. Craft a Graboid head (or purchase a small toy Graboid) with an open mouth, jagged teeth, and red accents.
  2. Mount it on a small wooden or foam platform, glued securely in place. Surround the base with faux moss, twigs, and sand to make it look like it's bursting through the "earth."
  3. Place the centerpiece in the middle of the table, where it acts as a thrilling and humorous conversation starter.
- Optional: Add LED lights under the Graboid for an ominous glow.

Option 2: Mini Desert Diorama

- Create a miniature Perfection Valley on a serving tray or shallow box using:
  - Fine craft sand or brown sugar for the ground.
  - Small faux succulents or cacti for desert plants.
  - Tiny toy trucks or figures to represent the survivors.
  - A small Graboid tentacle or head poking through the "ground" for dramatic effect.

Option 3: Seismic Lanterns

- Use rustic lanterns with sand-filled bases and LED candles. Attach small cracks, Graboid tentacles, or "seismic warning" labels to the outside of the lantern glass.
- Arrange three lanterns of varying heights down the center of the table for a simple yet striking look.

5.4 Place Settings: Where Graboids Meet Elegance

Your guests will appreciate the attention to detail when they sit down to enjoy the feast. Here's how to create cohesive *Tremors*-themed place settings:

Step 1: Plates and Chargers

- Start with **earth-tone chargers** (matte brown, black, or sand-colored) as the base.
- Use **white or beige plates** with subtle cracks drawn on them using food-safe markers or paint. For a playful twist, position small toy Graboid heads or tentacles sticking out from under napkins.

Step 2: Napkins and Napkin Rings

- Use **burlap napkins** or solid brown cloth napkins to keep with the earthy aesthetic.
- Create napkin rings using twine or miniature "seismic warning signs." Cut small rectangles from cardstock, paint them yellow with black stripes, and write phrases like **"CAUTION: GRABOIDS PRESENT."**

Step 3: Utensils and Drinkware

- Wrap utensils in twine or burlap and place them neatly on the napkin. For a fun touch, glue small plastic toy worms to the twine so it looks like the utensils are "under attack."
- Use mason jars or rustic glassware for drinks. Attach "Perfection Valley Water" labels to the jars for a clever nod to the desert setting.

Step 4: Name Cards

- Cut name cards into the shape of **seismic warning signs** or miniature desert rocks. Write each guest's name in bold lettering and place the cards on top of the plates.
- For added flair, scatter small faux pebbles or moss around each card.

5.5 Finishing Touches: Adding Atmosphere

To complete your *Tremors*-inspired table setting, incorporate small decorative details that tie the theme together:

1. **Sand and Rocks**: Lightly scatter fine craft sand, small pebbles, and faux moss along the table for a desert feel.
2. **Toy Trucks and Figures**: Place miniature trucks, toy soldiers, or small "survivor" figures near the centerpiece to add a sense of storytelling.
3. **Warm LED Lighting**: Weave warm white or flickering LED lights along the center of the table for a soft glow. Tuck the lights into moss or sand for a more organic look.
4. **Sound Effects**: For a playful touch, play *Tremors* soundtracks or add subtle seismic "rumbling" sound effects from a hidden speaker to immerse your guests in the experience.

5.6 A Feast to Remember

Once your table is set, it's time to serve food and drinks that match the theme. While we'll cover Graboid-inspired treats in Chapter 6, here are a few quick ideas to complement your table décor:

- **"Worm Tunnels"**: Spaghetti or pasta dishes served in a sand-colored bowl.
- **"Perfection Valley Dirt Cake"**: Chocolate pudding topped with crushed cookies and gummy worms.
- **"Seismic Cocktails"**: Drinks served with red and orange swirls to mimic desert sunsets.

Conclusion: Dining with the Graboids

Your *Tremors* table setting is now complete—a thrilling fusion of desert-inspired design, festive flair, and monster madness. By blending earthy textures, Graboid-themed centerpieces, and clever details, you've created a dining experience that's as immersive as it is unforgettable. Whether your guests are die-hard *Tremors* fans or newcomers to Perfection Valley, they'll be delighted by your creativity and attention to detail.

Chapter 6: DIY Graboid Snow Globes

No holiday décor collection is complete without snow globes. These classic, whimsical decorations encapsulate the charm and wonder of the season. But in *Tremors Wonderland*, snow globes aren't about serene villages or falling snow—they're about seismic chaos, swirling sand, and the terrifying emergence of Graboids beneath the earth. In this chapter, you'll learn how to craft **DIY Graboid Snow Globes** that feature mini desert-scapes, shaking Graboids, and a unique twist on the traditional snow globe concept.

With their eerie, desert-like beauty, these handmade globes are perfect for holiday centerpieces, mantel decorations, or themed gifts for *Tremors* fans. Let's shake things up!

6.1 The Concept: Turning Snow into Sandstorms

Unlike traditional snow globes filled with fluffy "snow," our Graboid globes focus on sandy, desert landscapes and monsters bursting through the terrain. Instead of winter serenity, you'll create scenes of suspense—Graboids rising, tunnels cracking, and sandstorms swirling ominously when shaken.

The best part? These globes are easy to make and endlessly customizable to suit your *Tremors* theme.

6.2 Materials Needed

To create your DIY Graboid Snow Globes, gather the following materials:

For the Globe

- Clear glass or plastic jars with lids (mason jars, old snow globe bases, or clear craft containers)
- Craft glue or a hot glue gun
- Sand or fine brown sugar (to mimic desert sand)
- Glycerin (optional, to slow the sand movement)
- Water (optional, if you prefer a wet globe)

For the Desert Scene

- Miniature toy Graboids or DIY clay Graboid figures (instructions included below)
- Small twigs, faux moss, or pebbles (for added terrain detail)
- Mini toy trucks, cacti, or survivor figurines (optional for storytelling)

For Decoration

- Brown, black, or red paint (to weather the base of the jar)
- Burlap, twine, or ribbon for wrapping the jar lid
- Fine glitter or small rocks for extra texture

6.3 Creating Your Graboid Snow Globe
Step 1: Crafting the Graboid

If you can't find miniature Graboid figures at a store, don't worry—you can make your own!

1. **Materials**: Use air-dry clay, polymer clay, or brown felt to create small Graboid heads.
2. **Shape the Body**: Roll the clay into worm-like shapes about 2–3 inches long. Leave one end tapered and slightly curled for realism.
3. **The Mouth**: Flatten one end of the worm and sculpt it into an open mouth. Add jagged "teeth" with small pieces of white clay. Use red clay or paint for the tongue and interior of the mouth.
4. **Detailing**: Add ridges or lines with a toothpick to mimic Graboid texture. Bake the clay (if needed) and paint it with shades of brown, black, and red for a rugged, monster-like look.

If sculpting isn't for you, substitute with toy worms or rubber snake toys cut and painted to resemble Graboids.

Step 2: Preparing the Globe Base

1. **Add Sand**: Pour a small amount of fine craft sand or brown sugar into the base of your jar. This will serve as the "desert ground." Use enough to cover the bottom while leaving space for other elements.
2. **Attach Terrain Details**:
   - Glue small pebbles, twigs, or faux moss to the inside of the lid or base of the jar to simulate a rugged desert scene.
   - Optional: Add small toy trucks, miniature cacti, or survivor figurines for storytelling. Position them as if they're fleeing the Graboid's attack.
3. **Add the Graboid**: Glue the Graboid figure in place, ensuring its mouth or tentacles are bursting through the sand. Tilt it slightly for a dynamic, rising-out-of-the-ground effect.

Step 3: Assembling the Globe

Choose whether you want your snow globe to be dry (with swirling sand) or wet (with suspended sand):

Option 1: Dry "Sandstorm" Globe

1. Secure the Graboid and terrain elements to the inside of the lid or jar base. Allow the glue to fully dry.
2. Place the lid onto the jar and tighten it securely. Test by shaking the globe to ensure the sand swirls naturally around the Graboid.
3. Optional: Add fine glitter to the sand for an extra festive shimmer.

Option 2: Wet "Sandy Water" Globe

1. Fill the jar ¾ full with distilled water. Add a few drops of glycerin (available at craft stores) to slow the movement of sand and create a mesmerizing effect.
2. Carefully sprinkle a small amount of sand into the water. Be conservative—the sand should settle at the bottom but still swirl when shaken.
3. Glue the Graboid and terrain details to the inside of the lid. Seal the lid with hot glue to prevent leaks.
4. Turn the jar upright and test the swirling sandstorm effect. Adjust as needed.

Step 4: Decorating the Globe Exterior

1. **Wrap the Lid**: Cover the jar lid with burlap, twine, or sand-colored ribbon for a rustic finish. Secure with glue or a knot.
2. **Add Details**: Paint the lid or jar base with cracks, seismic warning signs, or subtle dirt-like weathering. Use black and red paint to create ominous fissures.
3. **Optional Tags**: Tie a small tag around the jar labeled **"Caution: Seismic Activity"** or **"Beware of Graboids!"** for added fun.

6.4 Displaying Your Graboid Snow Globes

Once your snow globes are complete, place them strategically throughout your *Tremors Wonderland*. Here are some display ideas:

- **Mantelpiece Décor**: Arrange the globes alongside your *Graboid Stockings* (Chapter 3) and a few desert-themed props for a cohesive look.
- **Table Centerpiece**: Place multiple globes of varying sizes in the center of your dining table, surrounded by faux sand, rocks, and mini LED candles for an atmospheric effect.
- **Bookshelves or Side Tables**: Add a Graboid snow globe to your bookshelves or side tables for subtle, spooky accents.
- **Themed Party Favors**: Create mini snow globes as take-home gifts for guests at your *Tremors*-themed holiday party.

6.5 Tips for a Perfect Snow Globe

- **Seal the Lid**: Always use hot glue to secure the lid tightly, especially for wet globes. This prevents leaks and preserves your work.
- **Test Sand Amount**: If you're making wet globes, start with a small amount of sand. Too much can cloud the water and obscure the details.
- **Add Variety**: Experiment with different Graboid poses, terrain features, and jar sizes to create a diverse and dynamic display.

Conclusion: Shaking Up Tradition

Your DIY *Graboid Snow Globes* are now ready to take center stage in your *Tremors Wonderland*. These unique, desert-themed creations add a playful yet chilling twist to traditional snow globes, bringing the thrill of Perfection Valley into your holiday décor. With their swirling sand, detailed terrain, and monstrous surprises, they're sure to captivate guests and become a cherished part of your themed celebrations.

Chapter 7: Gift Wrapping with a Tremors Twist

In *Tremors Wonderland*, the thrill doesn't stop with decorations and table settings—it continues all the way to the gifts under your "Seismic Tree." Wrapping gifts with a **Tremors Twist** is a creative and exciting way to extend the theme into your gift-giving experience. Whether you're preparing presents for friends, family, or fellow *Tremors* enthusiasts, this chapter will teach you how to design unique wrapping paper, craft monstrous Graboid gift tags, and even add subtle surprises that bring the underground terror of Perfection Valley to life.

7.1 The Concept: Subtle Horror with Festive Flair

The goal is to merge traditional gift-wrapping charm with the *Tremors* aesthetic—think desert tones, seismic warning labels, and surprise Graboids peeking out from the wrapping. Every gift will look like it's been delivered straight from the dusty heart of Perfection Valley.

Here's what we'll cover:

- DIY wrapping paper designs featuring cracks, sand, and Graboid shadows.
- Creative Graboid-inspired gift tags.
- Fun embellishments like ribbons, faux dirt, and small "seismic warning" signs.
- Wrapping techniques for maximum monster impact.

7.2 DIY Graboid Wrapping Paper

Why settle for store-bought wrapping paper when you can design your own? Creating custom paper lets you infuse a *Tremors* twist into every gift.

Option 1: Seismic Cracks and Shadows

1. **Materials Needed**:
   ◦ Large rolls of kraft paper, butcher paper, or plain brown wrapping paper
   ◦ Black and dark brown markers or paint
   ◦ Paintbrushes or sponges for shading
   ◦ Optional: Red paint for "danger" accents
2. **Step-by-Step Instructions**:
   ◦ Lay the brown paper flat on a table. Use a pencil to sketch cracks and fissures across the paper to mimic seismic activity caused by Graboid tunneling.
   ◦ Outline the cracks with black marker or black paint. Make the lines jagged and irregular for a realistic look.
   ◦ Use a sponge or paintbrush to shade the edges of the cracks with dark brown for added depth.
   ◦ Optional: Paint small red warning signs near some cracks that say **"Caution: Seismic Activity"** or **"Beware of Graboids."**
   ◦ Once dry, cut and use the paper to wrap your gifts.

Option 2: Graboid "Shadow" Wrap

1. **Materials Needed**:
   - White or beige wrapping paper
   - Black or dark gray paint/markers
   - Sponge or brush for blending
2. **Step-by-Step Instructions**:
   - Lay the paper flat and lightly sketch Graboid shapes or shadows on the surface. The shadows can look like worm-like figures lurking just beneath the paper.
   - Use black or dark gray paint to fill in the shadows, blending the edges with a sponge for a subtle, ominous effect.
   - For added fun, include a few "tentacle-like" shadows emerging from the bottom or sides of the paper.
   - Let the paper dry, then wrap your gifts. When finished, it will look like Graboids are tunneling just below the surface of the gift.

Option 3: Stamped Desert Scene

1. **Materials Needed**:
   - Kraft paper or sand-colored wrapping paper
   - Small rubber stamps or homemade potato stamps shaped like Graboids, cacti, trucks, or seismic warning signs
   - Ink pads (black, brown, and red)
2. **Step-by-Step Instructions**:
   - Cut potato stamps in the shapes of small Graboids, tentacles, and other desert-themed items. If you have rubber stamps, you can use those instead.
   - Use black and brown ink to stamp Graboids emerging from random spots across the paper. Alternate with small cacti, trucks, or "warning" symbols.
   - Add red stamps sparingly to create danger signs or cracks in the earth.
   - Let the stamped paper dry before wrapping your gifts.

7.3 Graboid Gift Tags

No gift is complete without a gift tag, and *Tremors*-themed tags can add that final monstrous touch. Here are three creative designs:

Option 1: Seismic Warning Tags

1. **Materials Needed**:
    - Yellow cardstock or thick paper
    - Black markers or paint
    - Scissors and hole punch
    - Twine or burlap string
2. **Instructions**:
    - Cut rectangular or triangular tags out of the yellow cardstock.
    - Write **"Caution: Seismic Activity"**, **"Beware of Graboids"**, or **"Danger Zone"** in bold black letters. Add black diagonal stripes along the edges to mimic hazard tape.
    - Punch a hole at the top of the tag and thread twine or burlap string for attachment.

Option 2: Graboid "Bursting Through" Tags

1. **Materials Needed**:
    - Brown cardstock or kraft paper
    - Small Graboid shapes (cut from felt, clay, or printed images)
    - Glue and scissors
2. **Instructions**:
    - Cut tags into standard rectangles or circles from the brown cardstock.
    - Glue small Graboid shapes or cutouts to the center of each tag, making it look like the creature is "bursting" out of the tag.
    - Write the recipient's name on the bottom of the tag with black or red ink.

Option 3: Desert Rock Tags

1. **Materials Needed**:
    - Smooth craft rocks or faux flat pebbles
    - White paint pens or markers
    - Twine or hot glue for attachment
2. **Instructions**:
    - Write the recipient's name and a phrase like **"From Beneath the Sand"** or **"Delivered by Graboids"** onto the flat rocks using white paint pens.
    - Glue a loop of twine to the back of the rock so it can be tied to the gift.
    - These tags add a tactile, desert-like element to your gift wrapping.

7.4 Creative Gift Embellishments

To take your gift wrapping to the next level, add creative embellishments that reinforce the *Tremors* theme:

- **Miniature Graboids**: Glue small toy worms or tentacle props to the top of gifts for a 3D effect.
- **Faux Sand**: Lightly sprinkle craft sand on top of the wrapped gift (glue optional) for a rugged look.
- **Twine or Burlap Ribbon**: Replace traditional ribbons with natural twine or burlap to match the desert aesthetic.
- **Cracked Earth Bows**: Paint bows with black and brown "cracks" to make them look like fractured earth.
- **Mini Seismic Signs**: Attach small cardstock signs to the ribbon that read **"Tunneling in Progress"** or **"Danger Below."**

7.5 Wrapping Tips for Maximum Impact

- **Hidden Surprises**: Place small toy Graboids or worms inside the gift wrapping so they "pop out" when the recipient opens the present.
- **Layering Effects**: Combine multiple techniques—like seismic crack paper with a Graboid tag—for a cohesive and impressive look.
- **Color Balance**: Stick to earthy tones like browns, yellows, and blacks, with small red accents for warning signs. This will tie the theme together without looking too chaotic.

Conclusion: Gifts Ready to Shake Things Up

With your *Tremors*-themed wrapping paper, gift tags, and embellishments, your presents will become an extension of your *Tremors Wonderland*. Each gift is a work of art—fun, creative, and filled with subtle nods to the monstrous chaos of Graboids. Whether they're sitting under the "Seismic Tree" or handed out at a themed party, these gifts are sure to leave a lasting impression on everyone lucky enough to receive one.

Chapter 8: Lighting Up Your Tremors-Themed Home

No holiday wonderland is complete without dazzling lights, and a *Tremors Wonderland* is no exception. But instead of traditional candy-cane lanes and icicle lights, your home will pulse with seismic energy, glowing with a monstrous charm inspired by the chaos of Perfection Valley and its lurking Graboids. In this chapter, you'll discover how to create **Tremors-themed light displays** that combine holiday magic with an underground horror twist. From indoor ambiance to eye-catching outdoor setups, this guide will help you incorporate creative lighting that captures the essence of *Tremors*.

8.1 The Concept: Seismic Glow and Monster Magic

The lighting design will evoke a mix of **earthquake energy** and **Graboid terror**, with glowing tunnels, ominous warning signs, and flickering lights to simulate seismic disturbances. Whether you're illuminating your living room, your porch, or your entire home exterior, the key is to combine rugged desert aesthetics with unsettling bursts of festive light.

8.2 Indoor Tremors-Themed Lighting

1. Flickering "Seismic Fault Line" Pathway Lights

Simulate the earth's cracking surface with glowing, jagged light effects along your floors, walls, or table edges.

What You'll Need:

- LED strip lights (warm white, red, or orange)
- Black craft tape or black marker
- Twine or burlap for aesthetic cover (optional)

How to Create It:

1. Lay the LED strip lights in jagged, crack-like patterns along your floor, hallway, or table edges. Arrange them to resemble seismic fissures opening up.
2. Use black craft tape to add shadowy "cracks" directly onto the wall or surface around the lights to enhance the illusion.
3. Set the lights to **flicker mode** or pulsate intermittently to simulate tremors.
4. Optional: Cover sections of the LED lights with burlap or twine for a rugged, underground look.

2. "Graboid Glow" Under-the-Floor Lighting

Create the effect of a lurking Graboid tunneling just below the surface by strategically placing lights under furniture or rugs.

What You'll Need:

- LED puck lights or battery-operated mini spotlights (warm white or red)
- Thin burlap or sand-colored fabric (to diffuse the light)
- Optional toy Graboids or tentacles

How to Create It:

1. Place the puck lights or mini spotlights under rugs, couches, or tables, angling the lights slightly outward.
2. Cover the lights with thin burlap or sand-colored fabric to diffuse the light and create a glowing "earthy" effect.
3. For added realism, place toy Graboid heads or tentacles near the light source to make it look like the creature is bursting up.

3. Glowing Seismic Signs

Transform ordinary warning signs into illuminated décor pieces to emphasize the *Tremors* theme.

What You'll Need:

- Cardboard, foam board, or pre-made warning sign props
- String lights (red, yellow, or warm white)
- Craft knife and glue

How to Create It:

1. Cut or paint warning signs onto cardboard or foam board with phrases like **"Caution: Seismic Activity," "Graboid Zone,"** or **"Danger: Tunneling Worms."** Use bold black lettering on a yellow or red background.
2. Attach string lights to the back of the sign so the light glows around the edges or through cut-out lettering.
3. Mount the signs on walls, above doorways, or near entryways to serve as illuminated focal points.

8.3 Outdoor Tremors-Themed Light Displays
1. Graboid Lawn Lights

Give the impression of Graboids tunneling through your yard by creating glowing trails of lights and monster-themed focal points.

What You'll Need:

- Rope lights or LED strip lights (warm white or orange)
- Plastic stakes (to hold lights in place)
- Foam or plastic Graboid heads/tentacles
- Faux rocks or dirt

How to Create It:

1. Lay rope lights in jagged, winding patterns across your lawn to represent Graboid tunnels moving underground. Secure them with stakes.
2. Place foam or plastic Graboid heads or tentacles at various points along the rope light path, simulating where the monsters have "emerged."
3. Scatter faux rocks or piles of dirt around the light trails to enhance the desert illusion.
4. Optional: Use red spotlights near the Graboids to add an eerie glow.

2. Seismic Christmas Tree Display

Turn your outdoor tree or shrub into a *Tremors*-themed "Seismic Christmas Tree" with clever lighting effects.

What You'll Need:

- Warm white and red string lights
- Burlap garlands or sand-colored fabric strips
- Mini LED floodlights (red or orange)

How to Create It:

1. Wrap the tree with warm white lights to create the festive "base glow."
2. Layer red string lights unevenly along the trunk and lower branches to simulate the ground shaking or cracks forming.
3. Weave burlap garlands through the branches for an earthy, desert aesthetic.
4. Position mini red or orange floodlights at the base of the tree, aiming upward to create a glowing "seismic warning" effect.

3. Illuminated Graboid Silhouettes

Bring monstrous Graboids to life with glowing silhouettes that are perfect for your lawn or porch.

What You'll Need:

- Black foam board or plywood (cut into Graboid shapes)
- String lights or LED strip lights (red or warm white)
- Hot glue gun or clips

How to Create It:

1. Cut out large Graboid silhouettes with jagged mouths and tentacles bursting outward. Use black foam board for lightweight displays or plywood for durability.
2. Glue string lights or LED strips along the edges of the silhouettes, making them glow in the dark.
3. Place the glowing silhouettes around your yard, near bushes, or next to "tunnels" you've created with rope lights.

8.4 Bringing It All Together: A Seismic Spectacle

To maximize the impact of your Tremors-themed light displays, consider combining several of these elements for a fully immersive experience. Here's an example of a complete **outdoor setup**:

1. **Graboid Lawn Lights**: Lay glowing tunnel paths across the yard.
2. **Emerging Graboids**: Position foam Graboid heads along the paths, illuminated with red spotlights.
3. **Seismic Christmas Tree**: Add a glowing, flickering tree centerpiece for a holiday touch.
4. **Warning Signs**: Place illuminated seismic warning signs at key spots, like near your walkway or porch steps.
5. **Silhouettes**: Add glowing Graboid silhouettes to the porch or around bushes for depth and dramatic flair.

For **indoor displays**, combine flickering fault-line lights along hallways with glowing seismic signs and under-the-floor Graboid lights for an immersive "the monsters are inside" vibe.

8.5 Safety Tips for Lighting Displays

- **Use Outdoor-Safe Lights**: If decorating outside, ensure your lights are waterproof and rated for outdoor use.
- **Secure Cables**: Use stakes, clips, or adhesive strips to secure cables and lights, preventing tripping hazards.
- **LED Over Incandescent**: LEDs are safer, energy-efficient, and less likely to overheat, making them perfect for creative setups.
- **Weatherproof Decor**: For outdoor Graboids and silhouettes, seal foam board or plywood with waterproof spray or outdoor paint.

Conclusion: A Tremors Wonderland That Shines

Your *Tremors*-themed lighting displays will turn your home into a glowing masterpiece of monstrous holiday fun. From glowing tunnels and seismic warning signs to Graboids bursting through the ground, your lights will capture the essence of Perfection Valley while spreading festive cheer. Whether indoors or outdoors, these creative lighting effects ensure that your *Tremors Wonderland* will be the highlight of the holiday season—and maybe even scare off a few "naughty" visitors!

Part 2: Tremors-Themed Food

Chapter 9: Graboid Guts Stew

What's a *Tremors Wonderland* without a hearty, monstrous meal to warm you up after all that decorating and crafting? Enter **Graboid Guts Stew**: a rich, flavorful holiday stew inspired by the underground terror of Perfection Valley. Packed with hearty vegetables, tender chunks of meat, and a broth as deep and earthy as the Graboid tunnels themselves, this stew is the ultimate comfort food for *Tremors* fans. And with fun, creative garnishes that mimic the gooey, slimy appearance of Graboid "guts," it's as playful as it is delicious.

9.1 The Concept: Hearty Meets Horrifying

This dish combines the essence of a rustic, comforting stew with playful elements that capture the chaos of Graboids. The stew itself features a rich, brown base with chunks of meat and vegetables representing the rugged terrain of Perfection Valley. The garnishes—"Graboid guts" made from colorful pasta, stringy cheese, or gooey sauces—add a touch of themed fun that's perfect for a holiday gathering or *Tremors*-themed party.

9.2 Ingredients
For the Stew Base

- 2 lbs beef chuck roast or stew meat (cut into 1-inch cubes)
- 2 tbsp olive oil
- 1 large onion, diced
- 3 garlic cloves, minced
- 4 large carrots, peeled and sliced into thick chunks
- 3 celery stalks, sliced
- 4 medium potatoes, peeled and cubed
- 1 cup mushrooms, quartered (optional for a "muddy" look)
- 4 cups beef or vegetable broth
- 1 cup red wine (optional for depth of flavor)
- 2 tbsp tomato paste
- 1 tsp Worcestershire sauce
- 1 tsp smoked paprika
- 1 tsp dried thyme
- 1 tsp dried rosemary
- Salt and black pepper to taste

For the "Graboid Guts" Garnishes

- Black or red pasta (dyed spaghetti or fettuccine for a "tentacle" effect)
- Mozzarella cheese sticks (peeled into stringy pieces)
- Red and green bell peppers, sliced into thin strips
- Cornstarch slurry (2 tbsp cornstarch mixed with 2 tbsp water) to thicken the stew for a gooier effect

Optional Garnishes

- Crushed crackers or toasted bread crumbs for a "sandy" topping
- Fresh parsley for color contrast

9.3 Step-by-Step Instructions
Step 1: Sear the Meat

1. Heat olive oil in a large pot or Dutch oven over medium-high heat.
2. Season the beef chunks with salt and pepper. Sear them in batches until browned on all sides. Remove the beef and set it aside.

Step 2: Sauté the Aromatics

1. In the same pot, add the diced onions and cook until translucent, about 5 minutes.
2. Add the minced garlic and cook for an additional minute, stirring constantly to avoid burning.

Step 3: Build the Stew Base

1. Stir in the tomato paste, smoked paprika, thyme, and rosemary. Cook for 1–2 minutes to release their flavors.
2. Deglaze the pot with red wine (if using), scraping up any browned bits from the bottom.
3. Return the beef to the pot and add the carrots, celery, potatoes, and mushrooms.

Step 4: Simmer the Stew

1. Pour in the beef broth and Worcestershire sauce. Bring the stew to a boil, then reduce the heat to low and cover.
2. Simmer for 1.5–2 hours, stirring occasionally, until the beef is tender and the vegetables are cooked through.

Step 5: Add the Graboid "Goo" Texture

1. Stir in the cornstarch slurry to thicken the stew and give it a gooey, viscous texture that mimics Graboid guts.
2. Cook for another 5–10 minutes until the stew reaches your desired consistency.

9.4 Preparing the "Graboid Guts" Garnishes
1. Black or Red Pasta Tentacles

1. Cook black or red pasta according to the package instructions. (To dye pasta, add black or red food coloring to the boiling water.)
2. Drain and toss the pasta in olive oil to prevent sticking.
3. Drape the cooked pasta over the stew just before serving to resemble Graboid tentacles.

2. Stringy Mozzarella Cheese

1. Use mozzarella cheese sticks or a block of mozzarella cheese. Peel or shred it into long, thin strings.
2. Place the cheese over the hot stew just before serving. The heat will slightly melt the cheese, creating a gooey, stretchy effect that looks like guts.

3. Bell Pepper Strips

1. Slice red and green bell peppers into thin, irregular strips.
2. Scatter them across the top of the stew for a pop of color and a "slimy guts" appearance.

9.5 Serving Suggestions

- **Presentation**: Serve the stew in large, rustic bowls to emphasize its hearty, rugged feel. Let the Graboid garnishes hang over the edges of the bowl for dramatic effect.
- **Side Pairings**: Offer toasted garlic bread or crusty rolls for dipping, and a simple side salad with earthy greens to balance the richness of the stew.
- **Party Fun**: Place the pot of stew in the center of the table with a sign reading **"Beware of Graboids: Guts Inside"** for added thematic flair.

9.6 Variations
Vegetarian Version
Replace the beef with hearty vegetables like butternut squash, zucchini, or eggplant. Use vegetable broth and add beans or lentils for protein.
Spicy Graboid Guts Stew
Add red chili flakes, cayenne pepper, or hot sauce to the base for a fiery kick. Use red pasta for an even more dramatic effect.
Slow Cooker Option
Prepare the stew in a slow cooker for a hands-off approach. Sear the meat and sauté the aromatics on the stovetop first, then transfer everything to the slow cooker. Cook on low for 6–8 hours or high for 3–4 hours.

9.7 Final Touches

For an immersive *Tremors* dining experience, pair the stew with Graboid-inspired table settings (Chapter 5) and light up your dining area with flickering "seismic" lights (Chapter 8). Play the *Tremors* soundtrack or ambient desert sounds in the background for a fully themed meal.

Conclusion: A Feast Fit for Perfection Valley

Graboid Guts Stew is more than just a hearty holiday meal—it's a creative centerpiece for your *Tremors Wonderland*. Packed with rich flavors and playful garnishes, this dish is sure to delight fans of the franchise while satisfying your guests' appetites. Whether served as the main course at a themed dinner or as part of a casual holiday feast, it's a surefire way to bring the monstrous fun of *Tremors* to your table.

Chapter 10: Wormy Hot Chocolate Bar

A winter wonderland—especially one with a *Tremors* twist—wouldn't be complete without a decadent hot chocolate bar to warm your guests and delight their taste buds. But this isn't just any hot chocolate bar. In your *Tremors Wonderland*, the hot cocoa comes with a side of wiggling, wriggling fun: "worms" made from licorice and marshmallows that resemble Graboid-inspired toppings. This chapter will guide you in creating an unforgettable **Wormy Hot Chocolate Bar**, complete with rich cocoa recipes, creative toppings, and fun presentation ideas that will make it the centerpiece of your festive celebration.

10.1 The Concept: Decadent Meets Playful

The goal of your Wormy Hot Chocolate Bar is to blend traditional holiday indulgence with the playful, monstrous theme of *Tremors*. Picture a cozy spread of steaming mugs of hot chocolate topped with wriggling licorice worms, marshmallow "tentacles," and edible dirt sprinkles. This setup is perfect for kids, adults, and *Tremors* fans alike, offering a fun and interactive way to customize their drinks.

10.2 Setting Up the Hot Chocolate Bar

Before diving into recipes and toppings, create a space that's as inviting as it is thematic.

Designing the Bar

- **Tablecloth and Decor**: Use a brown burlap or sand-colored tablecloth to mimic the desert terrain of Perfection Valley. Add faux rocks, mini toy Graboids, or small cacti for decoration.
- **Signs**: Label your bar with a sign like **"Wormy Hot Chocolate Bar: Beware of Graboids!"** You can also create labels for individual toppings (e.g., "Edible Dirt," "Wormy Tentacles," or "Seismic Sprinkles").
- **Lighting**: Use warm fairy lights or flickering LED candles to create a cozy, welcoming glow.

Essential Equipment

- **Hot Chocolate Dispenser**: Use a large pot, slow cooker, or hot beverage dispenser to keep your hot chocolate warm.
- **Mugs**: Provide a variety of mugs, including some rustic or desert-themed designs to match the *Tremors* vibe.
- **Serving Tools**: Set out ladles, tongs, and small scoops for guests to serve themselves toppings and cocoa.

10.3 The Hot Chocolate Base

The foundation of your Wormy Hot Chocolate Bar is, of course, the hot chocolate itself. Here are two delicious recipes to choose from:

Classic Rich Hot Chocolate
Ingredients:

- 6 cups whole milk
- 2 cups heavy cream
- 2 cups semi-sweet chocolate chips
- ½ cup cocoa powder
- ½ cup sugar
- 1 tsp vanilla extract
- ¼ tsp salt

Instructions:

1. In a large pot, heat the milk and heavy cream over medium heat until warm (do not boil).
2. Whisk in the cocoa powder, sugar, and salt until fully dissolved.
3. Add the chocolate chips and stir until melted and smooth.
4. Stir in the vanilla extract and reduce the heat to low. Keep warm until ready to serve.

White Chocolate Hot Cocoa
Ingredients:

- 6 cups whole milk
- 2 cups heavy cream
- 1½ cups white chocolate chips
- 1 tsp vanilla extract

Instructions:

1. Heat the milk and cream in a pot over medium heat until warm (do not boil).
2. Stir in the white chocolate chips and whisk until melted and creamy.
3. Add the vanilla extract and keep warm over low heat.

10.4 Creative Graboid Toppings

1. Worm Toppings

- **Licorice Worms**: Use red or black licorice ropes. Cut them into various lengths (2–4 inches) and curl them slightly to mimic worms.
- **Gummy Worms**: For a fun, colorful twist, offer sour or regular gummy worms that can wriggle over the edge of the mug.

2. Marshmallow Tentacles

- **Classic Marshmallows**: Provide traditional marshmallows in various sizes.
- **Shaped Tentacles**: Use scissors to cut large marshmallows into thin, wiggly strips, resembling Graboid tentacles. Dust with cocoa powder or edible glitter for a festive look.
- **Toasted Marshmallows**: Use a kitchen torch or set up a small marshmallow toasting station for guests to roast their tentacles before adding them to their drink.

3. Edible Dirt

- **Crushed Cookies**: Crush chocolate sandwich cookies or graham crackers to create an edible "dirt" topping.
- **Brownie Crumbles**: Bake a batch of brownies, crumble them, and serve as a rich, fudgy dirt option.

4. Gooey Drizzles

- **Chocolate Syrup**: Offer classic chocolate syrup for guests to drizzle on top of their creations.
- **Caramel Sauce**: Add a touch of golden, gooey sweetness with warm caramel drizzle.
- **Red Raspberry Sauce**: Mimic "worm guts" with a tangy raspberry sauce.

5. Crunchy Add-Ons

- **Seismic Sprinkles**: Use red, black, and orange sprinkles to represent seismic activity.
- **Candy Rocks**: Offer candy-coated chocolates shaped like small pebbles to reinforce the desert theme.
- **Shaved Chocolate**: Set out a bowl of shaved dark, milk, or white chocolate for an elegant touch.

6. Whipped Cream Peaks

- **Classic Whipped Cream**: Serve a bowl of freshly whipped cream for guests to dollop onto their hot cocoa.
- **Festive Options**: Dust whipped cream with cocoa powder, cinnamon, or edible glitter.

10.5 Interactive Add-Ons

Encourage your guests to get creative with their drinks:

- **"Build Your Graboid"**: Provide small marshmallows, licorice strips, and candy eyes so guests can assemble their own Graboid creature on top of their hot chocolate.
- **Custom Flavors**: Offer mix-ins like peppermint extract, cinnamon sticks, or vanilla syrups to allow guests to customize their cocoa.
- **Graboid Mugs**: Use Sharpie markers to draw Graboid faces on plain white mugs before the event (or purchase themed mugs).

10.6 Presentation Ideas
Hot Chocolate Towers

- Use tiered trays or stacked plates to display your toppings in an organized, visually appealing way.

Thematic Jars and Bowls

- Serve toppings in jars labeled with phrases like **"Wriggling Worms," "Edible Dirt,"** or **"Graboid Tentacles."**

Mug Station

- Provide a variety of mugs with different colors and designs. Add a sign reading **"Choose Your Weapon Against the Cold!"**

10.7 Pairing Ideas

Pair your Wormy Hot Chocolate with other *Tremors*-themed treats:

- **Graboid Guts Stew (Chapter 9)**: Serve the stew alongside the hot chocolate for a full meal experience.
- **Dirt Pudding Cups**: Layer chocolate pudding, crushed cookies, and gummy worms for a fun dessert.
- **Monster Cookies**: Decorate sugar cookies to resemble Graboids or seismic warning signs.

Conclusion: Sweet, Warm, and Monstrously Fun

Your Wormy Hot Chocolate Bar is more than just a beverage station—it's an interactive experience that brings warmth, laughter, and a touch of monster madness to your *Tremors Wonderland*. With creative toppings, rich cocoa recipes, and a playful setup, this hot chocolate bar will be a hit with guests of all ages. So grab a mug, pile on the worms and marshmallows, and let the festive chaos flow!

Chapter 11: Graboids in the Snow: Cookies and Cupcakes

The holidays are the perfect time to indulge in sweet treats, and in *Tremors Wonderland*, desserts take on a monstrous, yet delicious, twist. Welcome to **Graboids in the Snow**, where cookies and cupcakes become miniature masterpieces of snowy chaos, featuring Graboids bursting through layers of icing and sugar. These desserts are sure to steal the show at your holiday gathering, offering a blend of creativity, humor, and delectable flavors.

This chapter provides detailed recipes for Graboid-inspired cookies and cupcakes, complete with snowy effects, bursting Graboids, and thematic decorations that are as fun to make as they are to eat.

11.1 The Concept: Sweet Monstrosities in Winter Wonderland

The idea behind *Graboids in the Snow* is to create desserts that depict Graboids tunneling through a frosty, snowy landscape. The cookies and cupcakes will feature:

- **Graboids bursting out of snowy icing**
- **Cracked earth designs with a frosty twist**
- **Creative use of edible decorations like candy, fondant, and icing**

11.2 Graboid Cookies
Ingredients
For the Cookies:

- 2 ½ cups all-purpose flour
- 1 tsp baking powder
- ½ tsp salt
- ¾ cup unsalted butter (softened)
- 1 cup granulated sugar
- 1 large egg
- 1 tsp vanilla extract

For the Decoration:

- White royal icing or frosting (for snow)
- Black, brown, and red gel food coloring
- Fondant or modeling chocolate (to sculpt Graboids)
- Small candy eyes (optional)

Step-by-Step Instructions
1. Make the Cookies

1. In a medium bowl, whisk together the flour, baking powder, and salt.
2. In a large mixing bowl, cream the butter and sugar until light and fluffy. Add the egg and vanilla extract, mixing until well combined.
3. Gradually add the dry ingredients to the wet mixture, mixing until a dough forms.
4. Divide the dough into two portions, wrap in plastic wrap, and refrigerate for at least 1 hour.

2. Shape and Bake

1. Preheat the oven to 350°F (175°C). Line baking sheets with parchment paper.
2. Roll out the dough to ¼-inch thickness and cut into irregular shapes, resembling cracked earth.
3. Bake for 8–10 minutes or until the edges are lightly golden. Let cool completely before decorating.

3. Decorate the Cookies

1. Use royal icing or frosting to create a snowy base on each cookie. Spread the icing unevenly to mimic natural snowfall.
2. Color small portions of fondant or modeling chocolate with black, brown, and red gel food coloring to sculpt tiny Graboids. Shape them into worm-like figures with open mouths and jagged teeth.
3. Place the Graboid figures onto the cookies, "bursting" out of the snow. Use candy eyes for an extra creepy effect.
4. Add red icing details to the mouths and cracks in the snow to simulate chaos.

11.3 Graboid Cupcakes
Ingredients
For the Cupcakes:

- 1 ½ cups all-purpose flour
- 1 ½ tsp baking powder
- ½ tsp salt
- ½ cup unsalted butter (softened)
- 1 cup granulated sugar
- 2 large eggs
- 1 tsp vanilla extract
- ½ cup whole milk

For the Frosting and Decorations:

- 2 cups buttercream frosting (white for snow)
- Black, brown, and red gel food coloring
- Licorice ropes (for tentacles)
- Chocolate chips or candy rocks (for "dirt")
- Edible glitter or powdered sugar (for snow effect)

Step-by-Step Instructions
1. Bake the Cupcakes

1. Preheat the oven to 350°F (175°C) and line a muffin tin with cupcake liners.
2. In a medium bowl, whisk together the flour, baking powder, and salt.
3. In a large bowl, cream the butter and sugar until fluffy. Add the eggs one at a time, then mix in the vanilla extract.
4. Gradually add the dry ingredients to the wet mixture, alternating with the milk, until just combined.
5. Divide the batter evenly among the cupcake liners and bake for 18–20 minutes. Let cool completely.

2. Frost the Cupcakes

1. Spread or pipe a thick layer of white buttercream frosting onto each cupcake to create a snowy surface.
2. Dust with powdered sugar or edible glitter to enhance the frosty effect.

3. Create the Graboid Effect

1. Sculpt small Graboid heads from fondant or modeling chocolate, similar to the cookies.
2. Place the Graboid heads on top of the cupcakes, partially submerged in the frosting. Position them at angles to mimic bursting through the snow.
3. Add licorice ropes as tentacles extending out of the frosting. Curl the ropes slightly for a dynamic look.

4. Add Finishing Touches

1. Sprinkle crushed chocolate chips or candy rocks around the Graboid to resemble dirt breaking through the snow.
2. Use red gel icing to add gory accents, like dripping from the Graboid's mouth or "cracks" in the frosting.

11.4 Presentation Tips
1. Snowy Dessert Display

- Arrange the cookies and cupcakes on a white platter or tray dusted with powdered sugar to create the appearance of a snowy landscape.
- Add small props, such as toy trucks or figurines, to simulate survivors escaping the Graboids.

2. Thematic Signage

- Label the desserts with fun names like **"Graboid Tracks"** (cookies) and **"Bursting Cupcakes"** to emphasize the theme.

3. Interactive Decorating Station

- Set up a decorating station where guests can create their own Graboid cookies or cupcakes. Provide pre-baked cookies and cupcakes, along with fondant, icing, and edible decorations.

11.5 Variations and Substitutions
Flavor Variations

- **Chocolate Cupcakes**: Add cocoa powder to the cupcake batter for a rich chocolate base that contrasts beautifully with the snowy frosting.
- **Spiced Cupcakes**: Add cinnamon, nutmeg, and ginger to the batter for a warm, festive flavor.

Dietary Adjustments

- Use gluten-free flour and plant-based butter and milk for a gluten-free and dairy-free version.
- Substitute fondant with fruit leather or vegan modeling chocolate for a plant-based alternative.

Conclusion: Monstrously Sweet Creations

With *Graboids in the Snow* cookies and cupcakes, you've turned traditional holiday desserts into show-stopping creations that combine sweetness with a playful *Tremors* twist. These treats are perfect for holiday parties, themed movie nights, or simply indulging in a bit of festive fun. Whether you're sculpting Graboids, decorating snowy landscapes, or letting guests unleash their creativity at a decorating station, these desserts are sure to be a hit.

Chapter 12: "Seismic" Spiced Punch

No *Tremors Wonderland* celebration is complete without a signature festive drink that perfectly embodies the energy and chaos of Graboids tunneling beneath the earth. Enter **"Seismic" Spiced Punch**: a flavorful, interactive beverage with a "shake-it-up" theme that's as fun to serve as it is to sip. This punch brings together warming spices, vibrant colors, and a hint of fizz, creating a drink that feels festive while aligning with the seismic excitement of Perfection Valley.

In this chapter, you'll learn how to create this show-stopping punch, complete with detailed recipes for both alcoholic and non-alcoholic versions, creative garnishes, and tips for an interactive serving setup that gets everyone involved.

12.1 The Concept: A Drink That Shakes Things Up

The essence of *"Seismic" Spiced Punch* lies in its presentation. Much like an earthquake shakes the ground, this punch comes alive when you "shake it up," blending layers of flavors and colors for an eye-catching effect.

- **Flavor Profile**: Warm spices like cinnamon, cloves, and star anise combined with citrus, cranberry, and a fizzy kick.
- **Visual Appeal**: Layers of deep reds and oranges mimic seismic activity, while garnishes and presentation add a Graboid twist.
- **Interactive Fun**: Guests can give their punch a shake (or stir) to unleash its full flavor and create a mesmerizing "seismic" swirl.

12.2 Ingredients
For the Base Punch (Serves 10-12)

- 4 cups cranberry juice
- 2 cups orange juice (freshly squeezed preferred)
- 1 cup pineapple juice
- 1 cup spiced apple cider
- 1 cup ginger ale (for fizz)
- 1 cup sparkling water or club soda
- ½ cup pomegranate juice (optional, for deeper color)

For the Spiced Syrup

- 1 cup water
- 1 cup granulated sugar
- 2 cinnamon sticks
- 5 whole cloves
- 3 star anise pods
- Zest of 1 orange

For the Garnishes

- Orange slices
- Fresh cranberries
- Cinnamon sticks
- Edible glitter or gold dust (for a festive shimmer)
- Optional: Gummy worms or licorice ropes for a Graboid twist

For the Alcoholic Version

- 1 cup dark spiced rum, bourbon, or whiskey (adjust to taste)

12.3 Step-by-Step Instructions
Step 1: Make the Spiced Syrup

1. In a small saucepan, combine water, sugar, cinnamon sticks, cloves, star anise, and orange zest.
2. Bring to a boil, stirring until the sugar dissolves. Reduce the heat to low and simmer for 5 minutes to infuse the syrup with spice.
3. Remove from heat and let cool. Strain out the spices and zest, and set the syrup aside.

Step 2: Prepare the Punch Base

1. In a large punch bowl or pitcher, combine cranberry juice, orange juice, pineapple juice, spiced apple cider, and pomegranate juice (if using).
2. Stir in the cooled spiced syrup, adjusting the amount to taste (start with ½ cup and add more for stronger flavor).

Step 3: Add the Fizz

1. Just before serving, pour in the ginger ale and sparkling water or club soda for a fizzy kick. Stir gently to combine.

Step 4: Chill and Garnish

1. Add orange slices, fresh cranberries, and cinnamon sticks to the punch for visual appeal.
2. Sprinkle a small amount of edible glitter or gold dust over the surface for a shimmering, seismic effect.

12.4 Serving Suggestions
1. Interactive "Shake-It-Up" Station
To emphasize the seismic theme, create an interactive punch station where guests can mix their own drinks:

1. Provide clear jars or glasses with lids. Pre-fill each jar with a portion of the punch base, leaving room for garnishes and fizz.
2. Set up a topping bar with garnishes like gummy worms, orange slices, cranberries, and cinnamon sticks.
3. Add a small shaker of edible glitter or gold dust for guests to sprinkle into their jars.
4. Encourage guests to "shake it up" before opening their jars to unleash the fizz and blend the flavors.

2. Graboid-Inspired Glasses

- Decorate glass rims with red or black sugar to mimic Graboid mouths.
- Add a small gummy worm or licorice strip to each glass, dangling over the rim like a tentacle.

3. Themed Ice Cubes

- Freeze cranberry juice or pomegranate juice in ice cube trays for dramatic red cubes that won't dilute the punch.
- Add small edible decorations, like cranberries or mint leaves, to the ice cubes for extra flair.

12.5 Variations and Customizations
Non-Alcoholic Version

- Follow the base recipe and omit the alcohol.
- Add extra ginger ale or sparkling water for additional fizz.

Spicy Citrus Punch

- Add a sliced jalapeño to the spiced syrup for a subtle kick of heat. Remove the jalapeño after steeping to avoid overpowering the punch.

Frozen "Seismic" Punch

- Freeze portions of the punch base in ice cube trays. Blend the frozen cubes with a splash of sparkling water or ginger ale for a slushy version of the punch.

12.6 Presentation Tips
1. The Seismic Punch Bowl

- Serve the punch in a large clear bowl to showcase its vibrant colors and garnishes.
- Place the bowl on a base of faux rocks or sand-colored fabric to mimic a desert landscape.

2. Thematic Signage

- Add a sign reading **"Seismic Punch: Shake to Activate!"** or **"Tremors-Themed Brew"** near the serving area.

3. Glowing Effect

- Place LED lights or a light-up drink tray under the punch bowl for a glowing, earthquake-like effect.

12.7 Pairing Suggestions

Pair *Seismic Spiced Punch* with other *Tremors* treats for a cohesive menu:

- **Graboids in the Snow (Chapter 11)**: Cookies and cupcakes are perfect sweet accompaniments.
- **Graboid Guts Stew (Chapter 9)**: Serve the punch alongside a hearty stew for a complete meal.
- **Wormy Hot Chocolate (Chapter 10)**: Offer the punch as a lighter alternative to hot chocolate for guests who prefer something refreshing.

Conclusion: Shaking Up Holiday Drinks

"Seismic" Spiced Punch is more than just a festive drink—it's an interactive experience that ties perfectly into your *Tremors Wonderland* theme. With its bold flavors, dramatic presentation, and "shake-it-up" appeal, this punch is sure to be a hit with guests of all ages. Whether served as part of a holiday party, a themed movie night, or simply to brighten a cold winter evening, it brings warmth, fun, and a touch of monstrous flair to your celebration.

Chapter 13: Tentacle Breadsticks

In the world of *Tremors Wonderland*, even the breadsticks get a monstrous makeover. **Tentacle Breadsticks** are a playful, delicious addition to your themed menu. These twisted, buttery breadsticks are baked to resemble Graboid tentacles, complete with texture and shape that bring the underground terror of Graboids to life on your dining table. Whether served as an appetizer, a side dish to accompany **Graboid Guts Stew**, or as a standalone snack for a movie marathon, these breadsticks are sure to delight and impress your guests.

13.1 The Concept: Edible Tentacles .

The idea is to create breadsticks that mimic the twisted, segmented appearance of Graboid tentacles. You'll use simple bread dough, add creative twists for texture, and bake them to golden perfection. For added flair, you can use colored seasonings, cheese, or herbs to highlight the ridges and details of the tentacles.

13.2 Ingredients

For the Breadsticks

- 2 ¼ tsp (1 packet) active dry yeast
- 1 cup warm water (110°F/45°C)
- 2 tbsp granulated sugar
- 3 cups all-purpose flour (plus extra for dusting)
- 1 tsp salt
- 3 tbsp olive oil

For the Tentacle Effect

- 2 tbsp melted butter
- 1 tsp garlic powder
- 1 tsp onion powder
- 1 tsp smoked paprika (optional, for color)
- ½ cup grated Parmesan cheese (optional, for texture)
- Fresh or dried herbs like oregano, parsley, or rosemary (optional, for decoration)

13.3 Step-by-Step Instructions
Step 1: Make the Dough

1. **Activate the Yeast**:
   - In a small bowl, combine the warm water, yeast, and sugar. Stir gently and let it sit for 5–10 minutes until frothy.
2. **Mix the Dough**:
   - In a large mixing bowl, combine the flour and salt. Add the activated yeast mixture and olive oil. Mix until a dough forms.
3. **Knead the Dough**:
   - Transfer the dough to a lightly floured surface and knead for 8–10 minutes until it becomes smooth and elastic.
4. **Let It Rise**:
   - Place the dough in a greased bowl, cover with a damp cloth or plastic wrap, and let it rise in a warm place for about 1 hour, or until it doubles in size.

Step 2: Shape the Tentacle Breadsticks

1. **Prepare the Dough**:
   - Preheat your oven to 400°F (200°C) and line a baking sheet with parchment paper.
   - Punch down the risen dough and divide it into 12 equal portions.
2. **Shape the Tentacles**:
   - Roll each portion into a long rope, about 12 inches in length.
   - Twist each rope loosely to create a wavy, irregular tentacle shape. For added realism, taper one end of each breadstick to resemble the pointed tip of a Graboid tentacle.
3. **Add Details**:
   - Use a knife or kitchen scissors to make small slits or indentations along the length of the tentacle for texture.
   - Brush each breadstick lightly with melted butter and sprinkle with garlic powder, onion powder, and smoked paprika for color.
4. **Decorate with Herbs and Cheese**:
   - If desired, sprinkle grated Parmesan cheese and herbs over the breadsticks to add texture and flavor.

Step 3: Bake the Breadsticks

1. Place the prepared breadsticks on the lined baking sheet, spacing them evenly.
2. Bake for 12–15 minutes, or until the breadsticks are golden brown and slightly crispy on the edges.
3. Remove from the oven and brush with additional melted butter for a glossy finish.

13.4 Serving Suggestions
1. As a Side Dish

- Serve the Tentacle Breadsticks alongside **Graboid Guts Stew (Chapter 9)** or a hearty soup for a delicious pairing.
- Place the breadsticks in a basket lined with a burlap cloth to enhance the rustic, desert-inspired theme.

2. With Dipping Sauces

- Offer a variety of dips to complement the breadsticks:
    - **"Graboid Goo"**: A warm marinara or tomato sauce.
    - **"Seismic Cheese Dip"**: A creamy cheese sauce with a hint of spice.
    - **"Worm Tunnel Ranch"**: A classic ranch dressing with added herbs.

3. Thematic Display

- Arrange the breadsticks on a platter with faux sand (crumbled crackers or breadcrumbs) and small toy Graboids for a playful presentation.

13.5 Variations and Customizations
Spicy Tentacle Breadsticks

- Add red chili flakes or cayenne pepper to the melted butter for a spicy kick.

Cheesy Tentacles

- Stuff the breadsticks with shredded mozzarella or cheddar cheese before twisting them into tentacle shapes.

Herbed Tentacles

- Mix fresh chopped herbs like rosemary, thyme, and parsley into the dough for a fragrant, savory flavor.

Gluten-Free Option

- Use a gluten-free bread flour blend and follow the same steps, adjusting water as needed for consistency.

13.6 Presentation Tips
Interactive Setup

- Provide each guest with a breadstick on a small plate, along with a "seismic" dipping sauce of their choice.
- Label the sauces with fun names like **"Lava Cheese"** or **"Cracked Earth Marinara."**

Thematic Platter

- Arrange the breadsticks in a spiral or wave pattern on a large round platter to mimic the movement of Graboid tentacles.

13.7 Pairing Suggestions
With Main Dishes

- Pair with **Graboid Guts Stew (Chapter 9)** or a pasta dish like spaghetti to complete a hearty meal.

With Drinks

- Serve alongside **"Seismic" Spiced Punch (Chapter 12)** or **Wormy Hot Chocolate (Chapter 10)** for a well-rounded meal experience.

Conclusion: A Monstrously Delicious Creation

Tentacle Breadsticks are more than just a side dish—they're an edible centerpiece that brings the monstrous chaos of *Tremors* to your dining table. With their twisted shapes, flavorful seasonings, and playful presentation, these breadsticks are sure to be a hit with guests of all ages. Whether paired with stew, served as a snack, or dipped into themed sauces, they add a creative and delicious touch to your *Tremors Wonderland*.

Chapter 14: The "Desert Feast" Main Course

A *Tremors Wonderland* wouldn't be complete without a show-stopping main course to anchor your festive meal. The **Desert Feast** takes inspiration from the rugged terrain of Perfection Valley and the monstrous appetite of the Graboids. This main course features hearty dishes, bold flavors, and creative presentations that evoke the desert's warmth and *Tremors*-themed chaos while remaining deliciously festive.

This chapter provides detailed ideas for crafting a *Tremors*-inspired Christmas dinner, complete with recipes, serving suggestions, and tips to create a cohesive and memorable dining experience.

14.1 The Concept: A Hearty, Thematic Feast

The Desert Feast should feel both indulgent and rugged, evoking the survivalist spirit of the *Tremors* franchise.

- **Main Course Centerpiece**: A bold, protein-rich dish like roasted meat or a vegetarian alternative that steals the spotlight.
- **Side Dishes**: Creative accompaniments with desert-themed twists.
- **Presentation**: Plates and platters styled to resemble the arid, dusty landscape of Perfection Valley.

14.2 The Main Course
Option 1: "Graboid Roast Beast" (Herb-Crusted Roast Beef or Lamb)

A tender, slow-roasted beef or lamb roast, crusted with earthy herbs and spices, serves as the show-stopping centerpiece.

Ingredients:

- 3–4 lbs beef rib roast or leg of lamb
- 4 cloves garlic, minced
- 2 tbsp olive oil
- 1 tbsp Dijon mustard
- 1 tbsp rosemary, chopped
- 1 tbsp thyme, chopped
- 1 tsp smoked paprika
- Salt and pepper to taste

Instructions:

1. Preheat your oven to 375°F (190°C).
2. In a small bowl, combine garlic, olive oil, mustard, rosemary, thyme, paprika, salt, and pepper to form a paste.
3. Rub the herb paste generously over the meat. Place the roast in a roasting pan fitted with a rack.
4. Roast for 1.5–2 hours, or until the internal temperature reaches your desired doneness (135°F/57°C for medium-rare).
5. Let rest for 15 minutes before slicing.

Presentation:

- Arrange the roast on a platter surrounded by "sandy" crushed crackers and sprigs of fresh rosemary to mimic desert terrain.

Option 2: "Seismic Bird" (Spiced Roast Chicken or Turkey)

For a more traditional holiday main dish, opt for a spiced roast chicken or turkey. The seasoning should evoke bold, smoky flavors reminiscent of desert heat.

Ingredients:

- 1 whole chicken (4–5 lbs) or turkey (10–12 lbs)
- 2 tbsp olive oil
- 2 tsp smoked paprika
- 1 tsp cumin
- 1 tsp garlic powder
- 1 tsp onion powder
- 1 tsp chili powder (optional, for heat)
- Salt and pepper to taste

Instructions:

1. Preheat the oven to 375°F (190°C).
2. Mix olive oil and spices into a paste. Rub the mixture all over the bird, including under the skin for maximum flavor.
3. Roast the chicken for 1.5 hours (or turkey for 2.5–3 hours), basting occasionally with its juices.
4. Let rest for 10–15 minutes before carving.

Presentation:

- Place the bird on a bed of roasted vegetables (carrots, parsnips, and potatoes) arranged to look like rocky desert terrain. Add small toy Graboids for a playful touch.

Option 3: Vegetarian "Graboid Pie"

This hearty vegetable pot pie features a flaky crust and a rich, savory filling of root vegetables and lentils, perfect for vegetarian guests.

Ingredients:

- 1 tbsp olive oil
- 1 onion, diced
- 3 cloves garlic, minced
- 2 cups diced carrots, parsnips, and celery
- 1 cup cooked lentils
- 1 cup vegetable broth
- 1 tbsp tomato paste
- 1 tsp smoked paprika
- 1 tsp thyme
- 1 sheet puff pastry
- Salt and pepper to taste

Instructions:

1. Preheat the oven to 400°F (200°C).
2. Heat olive oil in a skillet. Sauté onion and garlic until fragrant. Add carrots, parsnips, and celery; cook until softened.
3. Stir in lentils, broth, tomato paste, smoked paprika, thyme, salt, and pepper. Simmer until the mixture thickens slightly.
4. Transfer the filling to a pie dish. Cover with puff pastry, crimping the edges. Cut small slits in the pastry for steam to escape.
5. Bake for 25–30 minutes, or until the pastry is golden brown.

Presentation:

- Use cookie cutters to shape the puff pastry into Graboid-like tentacles before baking.

14.3 Side Dishes
"Tremor Taters" (Twice-Baked Potatoes)

- Scoop out baked potato halves, mash the filling with butter, sour cream, and cheese, and return it to the potato skins. Bake until golden and bubbly.
- Garnish with a dollop of sour cream and chives arranged to resemble cracks in the earth.

"Graboid Grains" (Wild Rice Pilaf)

- Cook wild rice with sautéed mushrooms, toasted almonds, and dried cranberries for a rugged, earthy side dish.
- Serve in a rustic bowl with a sprinkle of fresh parsley.

"Desert Veggie Medley" (Roasted Vegetables)

- Toss carrots, parsnips, sweet potatoes, and Brussels sprouts with olive oil, smoked paprika, and rosemary. Roast until caramelized.
- Arrange the vegetables on a platter in swirling patterns to mimic seismic activity.

14.4 Sauces and Condiments
"Seismic Gravy"

- Prepare a rich, brown gravy with pan drippings from the roast. Add a splash of red wine and a pinch of smoked paprika for depth.

"Graboid Cranberry Sauce"

- Cook cranberries with orange juice, sugar, and a hint of cinnamon for a bright, tart accompaniment.

14.5 Presentation Tips
1. Thematic Plating

- Use sand-colored or rustic ceramic plates to serve the meal. Arrange dishes to mimic a desert landscape.

2. Table Decor

- Scatter faux rocks, cacti, and small toy Graboids across the table for a playful, immersive setup.

3. Interactive Elements

- Place small signs next to each dish with fun names like **"Tremor Taters"** or **"Seismic Bird."**

14.6 Pairing Suggestions
Drinks

- Serve **"Seismic Spiced Punch" (Chapter 12)** or a bold red wine to complement the flavors of the feast.

Desserts

- Follow the meal with **Graboids in the Snow (Chapter 11)** cookies or cupcakes for a sweet ending.

Conclusion: A Festive Feast Worthy of Perfection Valley

The **Desert Feast** is a celebration of hearty flavors and creative presentation that captures the rugged charm and monstrous fun of a *Tremors Wonderland*. With bold main courses, flavorful sides, and thematic plating, this meal transforms your holiday table into an epic culinary adventure. Whether you're hosting a full holiday dinner or a themed movie night, the Desert Feast will leave your guests delighted and satisfied.

Chapter 15: Graboid Popcorn Mix for Movie Night

No *Tremors* movie marathon is complete without a snack mix that embodies the chaos and fun of the Graboids. Enter **Graboid Popcorn Mix**, a sweet-and-savory treat that's as thrilling as the underground monsters themselves. With a blend of crunchy popcorn, savory seasonings, and bursts of sweetness from chocolate and caramel, this mix will keep your guests munching through every tunnel collapse and Graboid attack.

This chapter provides detailed instructions for making a Graboid-inspired popcorn mix, along with serving ideas to enhance your movie marathon experience.

15.1 The Concept: Chaotic, Delicious, and Thematic

The *Graboid Popcorn Mix* combines textures, flavors, and colors to evoke the seismic energy of Perfection Valley:

- **Popcorn**: The base, representing the cracked and shifting desert earth.
- **Sweet Additions**: Chocolate, caramel, and candy for a touch of indulgence.
- **Savory Crunch**: Pretzels, nuts, or cheese powder for salty contrast.
- **Thematic Garnishes**: Red and black candy, gummy worms, or licorice ropes to mimic Graboids and their tunnels.

15.2 Ingredients
For the Base Mix

- 8 cups popped popcorn (freshly made or store-bought)
- 2 cups mini pretzels
- 1 cup salted peanuts or mixed nuts
- 1 cup caramel corn (optional, for added sweetness)

For the Sweet Additions

- 1 cup mini chocolate chips or candy-coated chocolates (red and black for a thematic touch)
- 1 cup gummy worms (to represent Graboids)
- ½ cup red licorice ropes, cut into small strips

For the Savory Seasoning

- 2 tbsp butter, melted
- 1 tsp garlic powder
- 1 tsp smoked paprika
- ½ tsp onion powder
- ½ tsp salt

For Optional Drizzles

- ½ cup melted chocolate (milk, dark, or white)
- ½ cup melted caramel

15.3 Step-by-Step Instructions
Step 1: Prepare the Popcorn Base

1. **Pop the Popcorn**: If using fresh popcorn, pop 8 cups using your preferred method (air-popped, stovetop, or microwave). Spread the popcorn onto a large baking sheet lined with parchment paper.
2. **Add Pretzels and Nuts**: Mix the mini pretzels and salted peanuts with the popcorn, spreading everything evenly across the sheet.

Step 2: Season the Mix

1. **Make the Savory Butter**: In a small bowl, combine melted butter with garlic powder, smoked paprika, onion powder, and salt. Stir until well blended.
2. **Toss the Mix**: Drizzle the butter mixture over the popcorn, pretzels, and nuts. Use clean hands or a spatula to toss everything until evenly coated.

Step 3: Add Sweet Elements

1. **Incorporate Candy**: Sprinkle the chocolate chips or candy-coated chocolates, gummy worms, and licorice strips over the mix.
2. **Optional Drizzle**: For extra decadence, drizzle melted chocolate and caramel over the entire mix. Let it sit for 10–15 minutes to harden before serving.

Step 4: Combine and Serve

1. Once all the ingredients are added, transfer the mix to a large serving bowl or individual cups.
2. Garnish with extra gummy worms or licorice ropes for a dramatic, Graboid-like effect.

15.4 Variations and Customizations
1. Spicy Graboid Mix

- Add a pinch of cayenne pepper or red chili flakes to the butter seasoning for a spicy kick.
- Include spicy pretzels or cheese crackers for added heat.

2. Sweet Graboid Delight

- Use kettle corn or caramel popcorn as the base.
- Add white chocolate chips and mini marshmallows for a sweeter flavor profile.

3. Gluten-Free Version

- Use gluten-free popcorn and pretzels. Double-check candy ingredients to ensure they're gluten-free.

4. Nut-Free Mix

- Replace nuts with sunflower seeds or additional pretzels for a nut-free option.

15.5 Presentation Tips
1. Thematic Serving Bowls

- Serve the popcorn mix in a large bowl shaped like a "cracked earth" or lined with burlap for a desert-inspired aesthetic.
- Use individual snack cups with labels like **"Seismic Snacks"** or **"Graboid Munchies."**

2. Interactive Graboid Stations

- Set up a DIY popcorn bar where guests can customize their mix. Provide toppings like candy, chocolate, and savory seasonings in small jars or bowls.
- Include a sign reading **"Customize Your Graboid Snack: Sweet, Savory, or Both!"**

15.6 Pairing Suggestions
Drinks

- Pair the popcorn mix with **"Seismic Spiced Punch" (Chapter 12)** or **Wormy Hot Chocolate (Chapter 10)** for the perfect movie marathon combo.

Other Snacks

- Offer **Tentacle Breadsticks (Chapter 13)** or **Graboids in the Snow (Chapter 11)** cookies alongside the popcorn mix for a varied snack spread.

15.7 Movie Marathon Tips
1. Thematic Playlists

- Watch the *Tremors* movies in chronological order while munching on the popcorn mix. Create intermissions for guests to grab refills or explore the DIY popcorn bar.

2. Trivia Breaks

- Between movies, host *Tremors* trivia games. Offer small prizes like themed snacks or props for correct answers.

3. Cozy Atmosphere

- Set up a comfortable viewing area with blankets, pillows, and desert-themed decor.

Conclusion: The Ultimate Movie Marathon Snack
Graboid Popcorn Mix is the perfect blend of sweet, savory, and thematic fun, making it an essential part of any *Tremors* movie marathon. Its interactive elements, bold flavors, and playful presentation ensure that it will be a hit with guests of all ages. Whether you're watching the original *Tremors* or diving into the entire series, this snack mix will keep everyone satisfied and engaged throughout the adventure.

Chapter 16: Monster-Inspired Gingerbread Houses

Nothing captures the holiday spirit like building a gingerbread house, and in *Tremors Wonderland*, your gingerbread creation takes a monstrous twist. In this chapter, you'll learn how to craft a **Perfection, NV-inspired gingerbread house**, complete with the rugged charm and desert elements of the town where the *Tremors* chaos unfolds. This unique twist on a traditional gingerbread house will serve as the perfect centerpiece for your *Tremors*-themed holiday décor.

16.1 The Concept: A Gingerbread Perfection

The goal is to recreate the iconic, dusty desert town of Perfection, NV, in edible form. This gingerbread structure will feature:

- **Rustic Buildings**: Gingerbread modeled after Perfection's classic structures like the general store, Burt Gummer's bunker, and weathered houses.
- **Desert Landscape**: Use crushed cookies, edible rocks, and candy to create a rugged desert terrain.
- **Graboids**: Add licorice, gummy worms, or fondant to represent Graboids bursting through the earth.

16.2 Planning Your Gingerbread Town
Buildings to Include

- **Walter Chang's Market**: The centerpiece of Perfection, with a rustic wooden exterior.
- **Burt Gummer's Bunker**: A fortified structure with military details.
- **General Houses**: Small, simple gingerbread houses to fill the town.

Desert Details

- Include dirt roads, rocks, and sparse vegetation using crushed cookies, pretzel sticks, and green icing.
- Create Graboid tunnels with licorice ropes or piped chocolate.

16.3 Ingredients and Materials
For the Gingerbread

- 3 cups all-purpose flour
- 1 tsp baking soda
- ½ tsp salt
- 1 tbsp ground ginger
- 2 tsp ground cinnamon
- ½ tsp ground cloves
- ½ tsp nutmeg
- ½ cup unsalted butter (softened)
- ½ cup granulated sugar
- ½ cup molasses
- ¼ cup honey
- 1 large egg

For the Royal Icing (Edible Glue)

- 4 cups powdered sugar
- 3 tbsp meringue powder
- 6 tbsp water

For Decoration

- Crushed graham crackers or chocolate cookies (for "sand")
- Candy rocks or chocolate-covered almonds
- Red and black licorice ropes
- Gummy worms (for Graboids)
- Pretzel sticks (for fences or wood planks)
- Assorted candies (to decorate buildings)
- Edible glitter (for added flair)

16.4 Step-by-Step Instructions
Step 1: Make the Gingerbread Dough

1. **Mix Dry Ingredients**: In a large bowl, whisk together flour, baking soda, salt, ginger, cinnamon, cloves, and nutmeg.
2. **Cream Butter and Sugar**: In another bowl, cream the butter and sugar until light and fluffy. Add molasses, honey, and egg, mixing until smooth.
3. **Combine and Chill**: Gradually add the dry ingredients to the wet ingredients until a dough forms. Divide the dough into two portions, wrap in plastic wrap, and refrigerate for at least 1 hour.

Step 2: Create Building Templates

1. Use cardboard or stiff paper to create templates for the buildings. Include walls, roofs, and other structural details for Walter Chang's Market, Burt Gummer's bunker, and smaller houses.
2. Don't forget to add details like windows, doors, and rooflines to each template.

Step 3: Roll, Cut, and Bake

1. Preheat the oven to 350°F (175°C) and line baking sheets with parchment paper.
2. Roll out the chilled dough on a floured surface to about ¼-inch thickness.
3. Use your templates to cut out the gingerbread pieces. Carefully transfer the pieces to the baking sheets.
4. Bake for 10–12 minutes, or until the edges are firm. Let cool completely before assembly.

Step 4: Make the Royal Icing

1. In a large bowl, whisk together powdered sugar and meringue powder.
2. Add water gradually, mixing until the icing is thick but pipeable. Adjust the consistency by adding more powdered sugar or water as needed.

Step 5: Assemble the Gingerbread Town
1. Build the Structures

- Use royal icing to "glue" the walls of each building together. Let the walls dry and set before attaching roofs.
- Decorate each building with candies and icing to reflect its purpose:
    - **Walter Chang's Market**: Add candy signs and licorice trim for a rustic look.
    - **Burt Gummer's Bunker**: Use pretzel sticks for wooden reinforcements and candy rocks around the base.

2. Create the Landscape

- Spread a thin layer of royal icing onto your base (a sturdy board or tray). Sprinkle crushed cookies or graham crackers over the icing to create a sandy desert terrain.
- Add candy rocks, pretzel fences, and small green icing "shrubs" for realism.

3. Add Graboids

- Use red and black licorice ropes to create Graboid tentacles bursting through the desert. Position gummy worms partially buried in the cookie "sand" for added fun.

16.5 Advanced Details
Seismic Cracks

- Use melted chocolate to pipe jagged lines across the gingerbread base, mimicking cracks caused by Graboid tunneling.

Interactive Features

- Place small LED lights inside the buildings to illuminate the town.

Snow Effect

- Dust the gingerbread structures lightly with powdered sugar to give the appearance of snow in the desert.

16.6 Presentation Tips

1. **Display Base**: Place the gingerbread town on a large wooden board or a tray covered with burlap to mimic a desert setting.
2. **Signs**: Add small candy or cardboard signs labeled **"Perfection, NV"** and **"Watch for Graboids."**
3. **Interactive Fun**: Let guests add their own decorative touches or position gummy worms for a collaborative activity.

16.7 Pairing Suggestions

Serve your Monster-Inspired Gingerbread Houses alongside **Wormy Hot Chocolate (Chapter 10)** or **Seismic Spiced Punch (Chapter 12)** to complete the themed experience.

Conclusion: A Festive Tribute to Perfection

Your Monster-Inspired Gingerbread Houses are more than just a holiday decoration—they're a celebration of creativity, fun, and the unforgettable world of *Tremors*. By incorporating iconic buildings, a rugged desert landscape, and mischievous Graboids, this edible creation will captivate guests and serve as the centerpiece of your *Tremors Wonderland*. Whether you enjoy it as a crafting activity or a delicious dessert, your gingerbread Perfection, NV, is sure to be a monstrous success.

This visual Concept of a Monster inspired Gingerbread Village.

Chapter 17: Tremors-Themed Cake Centerpiece

The crown jewel of any *Tremors Wonderland* celebration is a dramatic and delicious **Tremors-Themed Cake Centerpiece**. This multi-layered masterpiece combines layers of cake, edible sand, tunnels, and realistic edible monsters to create a stunning visual and culinary delight. Whether you're hosting a *Tremors* movie marathon, a themed holiday party, or a dessert competition, this cake will capture the essence of Perfection, NV, and its subterranean chaos.

17.1 The Concept: Layers of Danger and Delight

The *Tremors*-themed cake brings the desert landscape to life with layers designed to tell a story:

- **Edible Sand**: Crushed cookies and sugar create the dry, cracked earth of Perfection Valley.
- **Tunnels**: Hollowed-out cake sections represent Graboid tunnels snaking through the layers.
- **Monsters**: Fondant, candy, or sculpted chocolate depict Graboids bursting from the cake, creating a sense of movement and drama.

17.2 Planning Your Cake Design
Key Elements to Include

- **Base Layer**: A large, sturdy bottom tier representing the desert floor.
- **Middle Layer(s)**: Tunnels visible through cutouts or edible decorations.
- **Top Layer**: A dramatic Graboid bursting out of the ground.
- **Decorative Touches**: Cacti, rocks, and sand-like textures for realism.

Color Scheme

Stick to warm, earthy tones like browns, tans, and reds, with accents of black (for tunnels) and green (for desert vegetation).

17.3 Ingredients and Tools
Cake

- 3 layers of your favorite cake (8-inch or 9-inch rounds work best)
- Buttercream frosting (neutral or brown tones)
- Fondant (brown, black, and red for Graboids and tunnels)

Edible Sand

- 1 cup crushed graham crackers or vanilla cookies
- 2 tbsp granulated sugar
- 1 tsp cocoa powder (optional, for darker sand tones)

For Graboid Decorations

- Modeling chocolate or fondant (red, black, and brown)
- Candy eyes or small edible decorations for Graboid faces
- Red and black licorice ropes for tentacles

Tools

- Offset spatula
- Piping bags and tips
- Small knife or sculpting tools (for tunnels and details)
- Cake turntable (optional, for easier assembly)

17.4 Step-by-Step Instructions
Step 1: Prepare the Cake Layers

1. **Bake the Cake**: Prepare and bake three 8-inch or 9-inch cake layers in your desired flavor. Let them cool completely before assembling.
2. **Level the Layers**: Use a serrated knife to level the tops of the cake layers for easy stacking.

Step 2: Make the Edible Sand

1. Combine crushed graham crackers, granulated sugar, and cocoa powder in a bowl. Mix until evenly blended.
2. Set aside to use for decorating the layers and creating the sandy terrain.

Step 3: Assemble the Cake
1. Base Layer (Desert Floor)

- Place the first cake layer on a cake board or serving plate. Spread a thin layer of buttercream frosting over the top to act as glue.
- Sprinkle a generous amount of edible sand onto the frosting to create the desert base.

2. Middle Layer (Tunnels)

- Use a small knife or round cutter to carve tunnel shapes into the second cake layer. Ensure the tunnels are visible from the side.
- Place the second layer on top of the first, aligning the tunnels. Fill the hollowed-out sections with black or brown buttercream to represent the interior of the tunnels.

3. Top Layer (Graboid Scene)

- Place the third cake layer on top. Use frosting to secure it. Smooth the sides and top with a thin crumb coat of buttercream.

Step 4: Decorate the Cake
1. Create the Desert Effect

- Spread a final layer of buttercream over the entire cake. Sprinkle edible sand over the top and sides, pressing gently to adhere.

2. Add Cacti and Rocks

- Sculpt small cacti from green fondant or modeling chocolate. Add brown and gray fondant rocks around the base and top of the cake.

3. Graboid Bursting Out

- Sculpt a Graboid head using brown or black fondant. Add jagged teeth and a red interior for its mouth.
- Position the Graboid on top of the cake, partially buried in edible sand. Add licorice ropes as tentacles bursting out from the ground.

4. Highlight the Tunnels

- Pipe dark frosting around the tunnel edges to create depth. Add edible rocks or candy around the openings for a realistic look.

17.5 Advanced Techniques
Lighting Effect

- Place small LED tea lights or glow sticks inside the tunnels to illuminate them, creating a dramatic effect.

Interactive Elements

- Add edible "danger" signs on toothpicks, labeling areas like **"Graboid Tunnels"** or **"Caution: Seismic Activity."**

Snowy Desert Option

- Lightly dust the cake with powdered sugar to give the appearance of snow in the desert.

17.6 Presentation Tips

- Serve the cake on a wooden board or tray covered in crushed graham crackers to extend the desert theme.
- Surround the cake with toy Graboids or small figurines for added flair.

17.7 Pairing Suggestions
With Drinks

- Serve alongside **"Seismic Spiced Punch" (Chapter 12)** or **Wormy Hot Chocolate (Chapter 10)** for a cohesive menu.

With Other Desserts

- Complement the cake with **Graboids in the Snow (Chapter 11)** cookies or cupcakes for a varied dessert table.

Conclusion: A Monster of a Cake

The *Tremors-Themed Cake Centerpiece* is more than just dessert—it's a visually stunning, edible tribute to the chaos and creativity of Perfection Valley. With its layered design, detailed tunnels, and Graboid accents, this cake will be the highlight of your *Tremors Wonderland*. Whether served as the grand finale of a themed dinner or the centerpiece of a holiday party, this cake is guaranteed to leave your guests amazed and satisfied.

Part 3: Tremors Movie Marathon

Chapter 18: Setting the Scene for Movie Night

The heart of your *Tremors Wonderland* celebration is the ultimate movie night, and setting the scene is key to creating an immersive and memorable experience. Whether you're hosting a full house of *Tremors* fans or enjoying a cozy night with family, transforming your living room into a *Tremors*-inspired space will elevate the binge session from casual to unforgettable. This chapter provides a step-by-step guide for decorating your living room to bring the world of Perfection, NV, to life, complete with monstrous touches, desert aesthetics, and cozy movie-watching essentials.

18.1 The Concept: From Living Room to Perfection, NV

Your living room should evoke the rustic, desert vibe of Perfection, NV, while incorporating playful nods to the *Tremors* franchise. The theme should balance comfort for movie-watching with dramatic, thematic décor that draws guests into the world of underground monsters.

Key Elements

1. **Desert Atmosphere: Create the arid, dusty feel of Perfection with neutral tones, sand-like textures, and natural elements.**
2. **Graboid Chaos: Add bursts of monster mayhem with Graboids "breaking through" walls, floors, and decorations.**
3. **Cozy Seating: Ensure all guests are comfortable with plenty of seating, blankets, and cushions.**
4. **Lighting: Use atmospheric lighting to enhance the mood, from desert sunsets to flickering "seismic" effects.**

18.2 Preparing the Space

1. Clear the Area

- Remove unnecessary furniture and items to create an open, uncluttered space for seating and decorations.
- Arrange seating to ensure everyone has a good view of the screen.

2. Protect the Floors

- Use rugs, burlap, or fabric to cover the floor and create a neutral, desert-like base. For added fun, sprinkle a small amount of clean, crushed graham crackers to mimic sand (optional and easy to clean afterward).

18.3 Thematic Decorations

1. Walls and Backgrounds

- **Desert Backdrop:** Hang beige or sand-colored fabric on the walls to simulate the desert terrain. Use brown or tan paper to create jagged "rock" shapes and tape them to the fabric for depth.
- **Seismic Cracks:** Use black masking tape or paint to create "cracks" on the walls and floor, simulating seismic activity. Add small toy Graboids or tentacles bursting through for dramatic flair.
- **Posters and Signs:** Hang *Tremors* movie posters or create custom signs like "Welcome to Perfection, NV" or "Beware of Graboids."

2. Furniture and Props

- **Rustic Furniture:** Use wooden crates, stools, or rustic tables to enhance the desert vibe.
- **Graboid Ambushes:** Place foam or cardboard Graboid heads "bursting" through tables or walls. Use black and red paint to add realism.
- **Toy Trucks and Figures:** Scatter small toy vehicles, cacti, and action figures around the room to evoke Perfection's survivalist spirit.

3. Desert Terrain

- **Edible Sand:** Fill shallow trays with crushed graham crackers or brown sugar and place them on tables for a tactile "sand" effect.
- **Faux Rocks:** Arrange lightweight foam rocks or crumpled paper painted gray and brown around the room.

18.4 Cozy Movie-Watching Essentials
1. Seating

- Arrange couches, armchairs, and floor cushions in a semi-circle around the screen.
- Add throw blankets in neutral tones for warmth and comfort. For a thematic touch, use burlap or desert-patterned fabric as covers.

2. Snacks and Drinks Station

- Set up a Tremors Snack Bar with Graboid Popcorn Mix (Chapter 15), Tentacle Breadsticks (Chapter 13), and Seismic Spiced Punch (Chapter 12).
- Label each snack with fun signs like "Graboid Tunnels" or "Perfection Bites."

3. Personal Touches

- Provide small lap trays or TV dinner trays for guests to place snacks and drinks.
- Offer themed coasters or napkins with *Tremors* quotes or imagery.

18.5 Lighting and Effects
1. Ambient Lighting

- Use warm fairy lights or string lights to mimic a desert sunset. Hang them around the room or drape them across furniture.
- Add LED candles for a soft, flickering glow.

2. Seismic Effects

- Create the illusion of seismic activity with flickering LED lights placed under furniture or behind decorations.
- Use a small speaker to play low, rumbling sounds periodically for an immersive experience.

3. Thematic Projections

- Use a projector to display desert landscapes or *Tremors* movie clips on an empty wall before the movie begins.

18.6 Interactive Elements
1. Photo Booth

- Set up a small area with a "Perfection, NV" backdrop and props like cowboy hats, toy Graboids, and survival gear for guests to take themed photos.

2. Trivia and Games

- Before the movie starts, host a quick *Tremors* trivia game. Offer small prizes like gummy worms or *Tremors* posters for correct answers.

3. Graboid Alerts

- Create small Graboid "alarm" props (lights or buzzers) that go off during intense movie moments. Guests can press a button to "warn" others of impending chaos.

18.7 Final Touches
Soundtrack and Atmosphere

- Play the *Tremors* soundtrack or ambient desert sounds before the movie starts to set the mood.

Welcome Speech

- Greet guests with a short, humorous welcome speech, reminding them to stay vigilant for Graboid attacks.

18.8 Cleanup Tips

- Use lightweight, reusable materials for easy cleanup, like fabric backdrops and foam decorations.
- Have trash bins easily accessible for guests to dispose of snack wrappers and cups.

Conclusion: The Ultimate Tremors Movie Night
With your living room transformed into a dusty, chaotic Perfection, NV, and every detail designed to enhance the *Tremors* experience, your movie marathon is guaranteed to be a hit. From desert-inspired decorations to cozy seating and immersive sound effects, you've

created a space that brings the world of Graboids to life. All that's left to do is grab your snacks, press play, and enjoy the underground chaos with your guests!

Chapter 19: The Tremors Movie Line-Up

No *Tremors Wonderland* celebration would be complete without diving into the entire *Tremors* movie series. With a mix of horror, comedy, and action, the *Tremors* franchise has entertained fans for decades, evolving its storyline and introducing new threats while keeping the spirit of Perfection, NV, alive. This chapter provides an extensive breakdown of the movies, exploring their plots, themes, and characters, along with recommendations for the best viewing order to maximize the experience.

19.1 The Movies in Chronological Order (Release Date)

Here's a quick look at the *Tremors* movies in the order they were released:

1. **Tremors (1990)**
2. **Tremors 2: Aftershocks (1996)**
3. **Tremors 3: Back to Perfection (2001)**
4. **Tremors 4: The Legend Begins (2004)**
5. **Tremors 5: Bloodlines (2015)**
6. **Tremors: A Cold Day in Hell (2018)**
7. **Tremors: Shrieker Island (2020)**

While this order reflects the franchise's evolution, watching them in narrative order (detailed below) provides a more immersive experience.

19.2 The Recommended Viewing Order

To fully appreciate the story's development and the introduction of new creatures, watch the movies in the following order:

1. Tremors 4: The Legend Begins (2004)

- Plot: This prequel takes viewers back to the late 1800s, showing the origins of Perfection, NV, and its first encounter with Graboids. The story follows Hiram Gummer, an ancestor of Burt Gummer, as he transitions from a city slicker to a survivalist.
- Why Start Here: It sets the stage for the *Tremors* universe, introducing the Graboids' initial appearance and Perfection's history.

2. Tremors (1990)

- Plot: The classic that started it all, this film follows Val McKee and Earl Bassett as they discover Graboids terrorizing Perfection. With a mix of humor and suspense, it establishes the franchise's tone and introduces iconic characters like **Burt Gummer.**
- Why Second: Watching this after the prequel shows the evolution of Perfection from a struggling town to the Graboid hotspot we know and love.

3. Tremors 2: Aftershocks (1996)

- Plot: Earl returns to battle Graboids and their new, more dangerous form—Shriekers—in an oil field in Mexico. With Burt's help, they confront the new threat in an action-packed sequel.
- Why Third: It expands the mythology of the Graboids, introducing their life cycle and evolution.

4. Tremors 3: Back to Perfection (2001)

- Plot: Back in Perfection, Burt takes the lead as Graboids return, evolving into Shriekers and then the aerial Ass-Blasters. This film adds humor and showcases the residents of Perfection adapting to life in Graboid territory.
- Why Fourth: It ties back to the town's legacy and sets up Burt as the definitive franchise lead.

5. Tremors 5: Bloodlines (2015)

- **Plot:** Burt teams up with his new sidekick, Travis Welker, to hunt Graboids and Ass-Blasters in South Africa. The film introduces an evolved Graboid species and shifts the action to a new location.
- **Why Fifth:** It revitalizes the series by exploring the global impact of Graboids and introduces new dynamics between characters.

6. Tremors: A Cold Day in Hell (2018)

- **Plot:** Burt and Travis travel to Canada to confront Graboids in the arctic. Burt's health becomes a subplot as he battles the creatures while facing his own mortality.
- **Why Sixth:** It adds depth to Burt's character and explores the adaptability of Graboids in extreme environments.

7. Tremors: Shrieker Island (2020)

- **Plot:** In this explosive finale, Burt faces genetically modified Graboids and Shriekers on a remote island. With high stakes and emotional moments, it serves as a fitting conclusion to the franchise.
- **Why Last:** It offers closure to Burt's journey and delivers a dramatic end to the series.

19.3 Movie-by-Movie Breakdown

Tremors (1990)

- **Key Characters: Valentine "Val" McKee, Earl Bassett, Burt Gummer, Rhonda LeBeck**
- **Notable Creatures: Graboids (introduced)**
- **Memorable Moments: The underground monsters' dramatic first appearance and the iconic pole-vaulting escape scene.**
- **Tone: Suspenseful, humorous, and character-driven.**

Tremors 2: Aftershocks (1996)

- **Key Characters: Earl Bassett, Burt Gummer, Kate Reilly**
- **Notable Creatures: Shriekers (introduced)**
- **Memorable Moments: Burt's over-the-top weaponry and the realization of the Shriekers' heat-sensing abilities.**
- **Tone: Action-packed and comedic with some horror elements.**

Tremors 3: Back to Perfection (2001)

- **Key Characters: Burt Gummer, Jodi Chang, Miguel, Melvin Plug**
- **Notable Creatures: Ass-Blasters (introduced)**
- **Memorable Moments: Burt getting swallowed by a Graboid (and surviving!).**
- **Tone: Campy and self-aware, embracing the franchise's humor.**

Tremors 4: The Legend Begins (2004)

- **Key Characters: Hiram Gummer, Christine Lord, Juan Pedilla**
- **Notable Creatures: Primitive Graboids (Dirt Dragons)**
- **Memorable Moments: Hiram's transformation from a clueless city man to a capable leader.**
- **Tone: A blend of Western and horror-comedy.**

Tremors 5: Bloodlines (2015)

- **Key Characters: Burt Gummer, Travis Welker, Nandi Montabu**
- **Notable Creatures: African Graboids (introduced)**
- **Memorable Moments: Burt's makeshift survival tactics and Travis's charm.**
- **Tone: High-energy with a modern action twist.**

Tremors: A Cold Day in Hell (2018)

- **Key Characters: Burt Gummer, Travis Welker, Dr. Rita Sims**
- **Notable Creatures: Arctic Graboids**
- **Memorable Moments: Burt's health struggle adds tension to his battle with Graboids.**
- **Tone: Tense and reflective, with bursts of humor.**

Tremors: Shrieker Island (2020)

- **Key Characters: Burt Gummer, Jasmine "Jas" Welker, Bill**
- **Notable Creatures: Genetically enhanced Graboids and Shriekers**
- **Memorable Moments: Burt's emotional farewell to the franchise.**
- **Tone: Darker and more intense, with a sense of finality.**

19.4 Viewing Tips for Maximum Fun

1. Plan the Schedule

- For a single-day marathon, allocate about 12–14 hours for all seven movies, including short breaks.
- For a multi-day binge, watch 2–3 movies per evening over a weekend.

2. Create Thematic Snacks

- Pair each movie with a themed snack from earlier chapters, such as Graboid Popcorn Mix (Chapter 15) or Wormy Hot Chocolate (Chapter 10).

3. Host Intermissions

- Between movies, host quick trivia rounds or Graboid-themed games to keep energy levels high.

4. Embrace the Atmosphere

- Use Setting the Scene for Movie Night (Chapter 18) to create an immersive viewing environment.

Conclusion: A Tremors Legacy Worth Celebrating

The *Tremors* movie series is a blend of humor, horror, and action that has captured the hearts of fans worldwide. By following this detailed viewing order and embracing the franchise's charm, you'll create an unforgettable movie marathon experience that celebrates the legacy of Perfection, NV, and its monstrous residents.

Chapter 20: Graboid Bingo: A Movie Game

No *Tremors* movie marathon is complete without an interactive game to keep everyone engaged. **Graboid Bingo** is the perfect way to turn your movie night into a thrilling competition. By spotting classic *Tremors* tropes, iconic moments, and quirky characters, you and your guests can immerse yourselves in the chaotic fun of Perfection, NV. This chapter provides detailed instructions for creating and playing Graboid Bingo, complete with printable ideas for bingo cards and suggestions for prizes.

20.1 The Concept: Movie Bingo, Tremors-Style

The premise of Graboid Bingo is simple: guests fill their bingo cards by spotting specific tropes, events, and quotes from the *Tremors* movies. From Burt Gummer's over-the-top weapons to a Graboid bursting out of the ground, the game celebrates the franchise's most iconic elements.

Why It Works

- **Interactive**: Keeps everyone engaged, even during slower scenes.
- **Thematic**: Highlights the unique humor, action, and characters that make *Tremors* special.
- **Customizable**: Cards can be tailored to the group's familiarity with the series or to specific movies.

20.2 Creating the Bingo Cards
Card Layout

- Use a standard 5x5 bingo grid with a free space in the center.
- Include 24 unique prompts related to *Tremors* moments, characters, or tropes.

Sample Prompts

Here are some ideas for bingo squares:

- **"Burt Gummer uses an absurdly large gun."**
- **"Someone says, 'We have to get out of here!'"**
- **"A Graboid bursts through the ground."**
- **"Shriekers detect someone using heat."**
- **"An Ass-Blaster flies into something and explodes."**
- **"Someone mentions Perfection, NV."**
- **"A Graboid tentacle grabs someone or something."**
- **"Burt complains about government incompetence."**
- **"A random character gets eaten by a Graboid."**
- **"A plan goes horribly wrong."**
- **"A truck gets stuck or breaks down."**
- **"A character sacrifices themselves heroically."**

- "An improvised weapon saves the day."
- "A Graboid gets blown up."
- "A map of the area is used."
- "A character shouts, 'Run!'"
- "Something is pulled underground by a Graboid."
- "A warning sign about danger is ignored."
- "Burt eats something while preparing for battle."
- "A character celebrates a narrow escape."
- "Someone sarcastically says, 'What could go wrong?'"
- "A Graboid appears unexpectedly."
- "An explosion solves the problem."
- "A character climbs something to avoid danger."

Designing the Cards

- Use simple graphics software or online templates to create the cards.
- Decorate them with *Tremors*-themed images, like Graboids, cacti, or desert landscapes.

20.3 Game Rules

1. **Distribute Cards and Markers**
   - Provide each guest with a unique Graboid Bingo card and a marker (stickers, pens, or small candies work well).
2. **Explain the Rules**
   - Guests mark a square when they see or hear the corresponding moment during the movie.
   - Only one square can be marked per moment. For example, if Burt uses a big gun, only mark **"Burt Gummer uses an absurdly large gun"**, not any related prompts like **"Burt complains about government incompetence."**
3. **Winning Conditions**
   - Traditional Bingo: A straight line (horizontal, vertical, or diagonal).
   - Full Card Bingo: Guests must fill every square.
4. **Challenges**
   - To keep things fun and fair, allow other guests to challenge questionable markings. For example, if someone claims Burt's weapon is "absurdly large," the group can debate its merit.

20.4 Enhancing the Experience
1. Thematic Prizes
Award prizes to winners to keep the competition exciting. Suggestions include:

- **Graboid Figurines**: Small toy worms or custom 3D-printed Graboids.
- **Themed Snacks**: Bags of gummy worms or popcorn in *Tremors*-themed packaging.
- **Merchandise**: *Tremors* posters, t-shirts, or DVDs.
- **Custom Coupons**: For things like an extra slice of **Tremors-Themed Cake (Chapter 17)** or a reserved seat at the next movie night.

2. Fun Announcements

- Use a small bell, buzzer, or light to signal when someone gets Bingo.
- Encourage winners to shout, "Graboid!" when they mark a full line.

3. Leaderboard
If you're playing across multiple movies, track who wins the most Bingos over the course of the marathon. Declare a grand champion at the end.

20.5 Customization for Different Groups
For New Fans

- Use simpler prompts, such as **"A Graboid appears"** or **"Someone climbs a rock."**
- Focus on prompts that occur frequently in the first movie to make the game accessible.

For Die-Hard Fans

- Include more obscure prompts, such as **"Someone mentions the Seismic Sensor"** or **"Melvin makes a sarcastic remark."**
- Add prompts specific to later movies, like **"A genetically modified Graboid is introduced."**

For Kids

- Include visual prompts with icons or illustrations for younger players.
- Use simpler language, like **"Worm comes out of the ground"** or **"Someone says, 'Run!'"**

20.6 Hosting Tips

1. Provide Clear Viewing Conditions

- Ensure the screen and sound are clear so everyone can spot Bingo moments easily.

2. Combine with Other Activities

- Pair Graboid Bingo with **Graboid Popcorn Mix (Chapter 15)** or **Tentacle Breadsticks (Chapter 13)** to keep the energy up.

3. Encourage Team Play

- Allow guests to form teams, especially if you're hosting a large group. This fosters collaboration and keeps the game lively.

20.7 Example Bingo Card

Burt Gummer Quote	Explosion Happens	Graboid Seen	Climbs a Rock	Hero Sacrifice
Truck Breaks Down	Map of Perfection Seen	Someone Screams	Shrieker Detected	Improvised Weapon
Plan Fails	FREE SPACE	Burt Eats Snack	Tentacle Grabs Someone	Graboid Tunnel Scene
"We Gotta Get Out!"	Melvin's Sarcastic Line	Cactus Seen	Heat Vision Used	Danger Sign Ignored

Conclusion: Turning Movie Night into a Game Night

Graboid Bingo transforms your *Tremors* movie marathon into an interactive and competitive event that everyone can enjoy. By blending iconic moments, clever prompts, and thematic prizes, the game adds a new layer of excitement to your *Tremors Wonderland*. Whether your guests are casual viewers or die-hard fans, Graboid Bingo ensures laughter, camaraderie, and a night to remember.

Chapter 21: The "Tremors" Drinking (or Cocoa) Game

Add a new layer of fun to your *Tremors* movie marathon with a **Tremors Drinking (or Cocoa) Game**! Whether you're sipping on hot cocoa, "seismic punch," or your favorite drink of choice, this game is the perfect way to keep the energy high and the laughter flowing during your binge session. In this chapter, we'll provide a detailed guide for creating a thematic drinking game tailored to the *Tremors* series, complete with rules, variations for non-alcoholic play, and safety tips to ensure everyone has a great time.

21.1 The Concept: Sip Along with the Chaos

The *Tremors* Drinking Game is designed to enhance your movie-watching experience by calling attention to classic tropes, iconic quotes, and memorable moments from the franchise. Guests take a sip (or bite, for cocoa drinkers) whenever specific events or actions occur. With each movie, the game builds on the hilarity and chaos that *Tremors* fans love.

21.2 Setting Up the Game

1. Choose Your Drink

- **Alcoholic Options**: Beer, wine, or cocktails. For themed drinks, use **Seismic Spiced Punch (Chapter 12)** or create custom Graboid-themed cocktails.
- **Non-Alcoholic Options**: Hot cocoa, sparkling cider, or soda. Add whipped cream or edible glitter for a festive touch.

2. Create the Rules

Decide how guests will drink:

- **Take a Sip**: For frequent or less dramatic events.
- **Take Two Sips**: For mid-level events, like new monster reveals or unexpected explosions.
- **Finish Your Drink**: For rare or game-changing moments in the movies.

21.3 Suggested Drinking Prompts

Here's a breakdown of events and actions that can trigger a sip, double sip, or finished drink:

Take One Sip

- A Graboid bursts out of the ground.
- Someone says, "We gotta get out of here!"
- Burt Gummer uses a new weapon.
- A character trips or falls while running.
- Someone climbs something to escape.
- A Graboid tentacle grabs someone or something.
- A loud explosion occurs.
- Someone sarcastically dismisses the threat.

- A map of the area is shown.

Take Two Sips

- Shriekers or Ass-Blasters appear for the first time.
- Burt complains about the government or survivalists.
- A plan completely fails.
- A truck or vehicle gets stuck.
- A Graboid is blown up in a dramatic way.
- A Graboid or Shrieker is unexpectedly smart.
- Someone uses a ridiculous improvised weapon.
- A character heroically sacrifices themselves.

Finish Your Drink

- Burt survives an impossible situation.
- A Graboid kills a major or beloved character.
- A new species of Graboid is revealed.
- A character delivers a classic one-liner, like Burt's **"I am completely out of ammo!"**
- The last Graboid or monster is killed.

21.4 Thematic Variations
Hot Cocoa Twist

For younger players or non-drinkers, adapt the rules to include sips of cocoa, bites of marshmallows, or even themed snacks:

- **Take One Sip**: Eat a mini marshmallow.
- **Take Two Sips**: Add whipped cream or toppings to your drink.
- **Finish Your Cup**: Top off your cocoa with a fun garnish like candy canes or sprinkles.

Graboid Snack Edition

Combine the drinking game with themed snacks, such as **Graboid Popcorn Mix (Chapter 15)** or **Tentacle Breadsticks (Chapter 13)**:

- **Take One Bite**: Eat a piece of popcorn or breadstick.
- **Take Two Bites**: Add toppings or dip your snack into a sauce.
- **Finish Your Plate**: Refill your snack bowl when major events occur.

21.5 Game Safety Tips
1. Know Your Limits

- Encourage players to pace themselves, especially with alcoholic beverages.
- Offer plenty of water and non-alcoholic options.

2. Designate a Host

- Have a designated host to manage the game and remind guests to drink responsibly.

3. Snack Often

- Provide plenty of food throughout the game to balance drinks and keep guests energized.

4. Alternative Rules for Kids

- Replace drinks with fun gestures, like clapping, cheering, or shouting, **"Graboid!"** when prompts occur.

21.6 Movie-Specific Prompts
For fans watching multiple movies, add prompts unique to each film:
Tremors (1990)

- Someone mentions Val and Earl's odd jobs.
- Rhonda talks about seismology or sensors.
- A Graboid takes out a fence or building.

Tremors 2: Aftershocks (1996)

- Earl laments about his post-*Tremors* fame.
- Shriekers attack in a swarm.
- Burt's military truck saves the day.

Tremors 3: Back to Perfection (2001)

- Burt eats something in the middle of a disaster.
- An Ass-Blaster causes an explosion.
- A Graboid is given a ridiculous name.

Tremors 4: The Legend Begins (2004)

- Hiram Gummer complains about manual labor.
- A Dirt Dragon attacks someone unexpectedly.
- Someone rides a horse to escape danger.

Tremors 5: Bloodlines (2015)

- Burt bonds with Travis.
- The South African setting leads to a new challenge.
- The Graboids exhibit new, terrifying abilities.

Tremors: A Cold Day in Hell (2018)

- Burt struggles with his health.
- The arctic setting presents an obstacle.
- A character learns about Burt's legacy.

Tremors: Shrieker Island (2020)

- Burt confronts a genetically modified Graboid.
- A character delivers a heartfelt speech about survival.
- The final Graboid attack is over-the-top.

21.7 Hosting Tips for Maximum Fun
1. Encourage Participation

- Share the rules before starting and provide printed cards or digital guides.
- Create a festive atmosphere with themed decorations and snacks.

2. Make It Competitive

- Award prizes for the best participant, such as themed merchandise, snacks, or movie memorabilia.

3. Combine with Other Activities

- Pair the drinking game with **Graboid Bingo (Chapter 20)** for an extra layer of fun.

21.8 Wrapping Up the Game

At the end of the marathon, congratulate everyone for surviving the Graboid-infested chaos. Consider a toast (with cocoa or cocktails) to celebrate the *Tremors* franchise and the unforgettable night you've created.

Conclusion: Sips, Laughs, and Monster Mayhem

The *Tremors Drinking (or Cocoa) Game* is a fun and engaging way to elevate your movie marathon. With a mix of iconic moments, hilarious tropes, and thematic drinks, the game ensures that everyone—whether sipping cocoa or cocktails—has a fantastic time. Just like the Graboids, this game will keep everyone on their toes, eagerly anticipating the next big moment.

Chapter 22: Monster Marathon Pacing Tips

Hosting a *Tremors* movie marathon is an epic undertaking, and pacing is key to ensuring your guests stay energized, entertained, and fully immersed. Whether you're watching all seven films in a single session or spreading them across a weekend, this chapter provides detailed tips for planning food breaks, intermissions, and activities to keep the fun going without overwhelming your audience.

22.1 The Importance of Pacing

A movie marathon is not just about watching back-to-back films; it's about creating a balanced experience. Proper pacing helps:

- **Maintain Energy Levels**: Well-timed breaks prevent fatigue and boredom.
- **Encourage Interaction**: Intermissions give guests a chance to discuss the movies, play games, or refuel.
- **Enhance the Experience**: Activities and themed breaks deepen the *Tremors* atmosphere.

22.2 Planning Your Movie Schedule

1. Consider Total Viewing Time

The *Tremors* series has a cumulative runtime of approximately **12 hours**. Plan your schedule accordingly:

- **Single-Day Marathon**: Begin early and include multiple breaks to sustain energy.
- **Multi-Day Marathon**: Watch 3–4 movies per day, splitting the series across two days or a weekend.

2. Build Breaks into the Schedule

- Plan **10- to 15-minute breaks** between movies for bathroom trips, snack refills, or quick discussions.
- Include at least one longer **30- to 45-minute meal break** for lunch or dinner.

22.3 Food and Drink Timing
1. Start with Light Snacks

- Begin the marathon with **Graboid Popcorn Mix (Chapter 15)** or **Tentacle Breadsticks (Chapter 13)** to keep guests satisfied without overloading them.
- Pair these with **Wormy Hot Chocolate (Chapter 10)** or a light punch.

2. Time Meals Around Key Moments

- Schedule a **major meal break** after the second or third movie. This allows guests to relax and refuel before diving back into the action.
- Feature a themed meal like **Graboid Guts Stew (Chapter 9)** or a **Desert Feast (Chapter 14)** to stay on theme.

3. Dessert and Coffee During Later Movies

- Serve **Graboids in the Snow Cookies (Chapter 11)** or **Tremors-Themed Cake (Chapter 17)** during the second half of the marathon.
- Offer coffee, tea, or energy drinks to keep guests alert as the marathon progresses.

22.4 Intermission Activities
1. Thematic Games
Use breaks for interactive games like:

- **Graboid Bingo (Chapter 20)**: A fun way to recap what's happened so far.
- **Trivia Contest**: Test guests on their *Tremors* knowledge with questions about characters, creatures, and plot points.
- **Prop Scavenger Hunt**: Hide small "Graboids" or other themed items around the room for guests to find during intermissions.

2. Stretch and Move
Encourage guests to stretch or walk around during longer breaks to avoid stiffness from extended sitting.
3. Social Discussions

- Create space for guests to discuss their favorite moments, characters, and quotes from the movies.
- Use thematic icebreaker questions, like **"Which *Tremors* character would you want on your survival team?"**

4. Photo Booth
Set up a **Perfection, NV-inspired photo booth** with props like cowboy hats, toy Graboids, and survival gear.
22.5 Managing Energy Levels
1. Hydration is Key

- Offer water alongside other drinks to ensure guests stay hydrated.
- Use themed water bottles labeled **"Graboid Fuel"** for added fun.

2. Create a Cozy Environment

- Provide blankets, pillows, and comfortable seating to keep guests relaxed.
- Dim the lights to create a movie-theater atmosphere, but keep the space warm and inviting.

3. Adjust the Temperature
If your marathon includes **Tremors: A Cold Day in Hell**, add a thematic twist by lowering the room temperature slightly or offering chilled drinks during that movie.

22.6 Thematic Intermission Ideas
1. Interactive Storytelling

- Create a quick Graboid-inspired survival scenario where guests must make group decisions to "escape" a fictional Graboid attack.

2. Graboid Crafts

- Host a mini crafting session where guests can make their own Graboid tentacles using licorice, fondant, or pipe cleaners.

3. Monster Documentary Clips

- Show short behind-the-scenes clips or interviews about the *Tremors* franchise during breaks to keep the theme alive.

22.7 Dealing with Marathon Fatigue
1. Allow Flexibility

- Let guests step out for breaks or skip a movie if they need a breather.
- Consider adding a pause button to allow everyone to regroup if the group energy dips.

2. Shorten the Line-Up

- If watching all seven movies feels overwhelming, focus on key entries in the series:
    - **Tremors (1990)**
    - **Tremors 2: Aftershocks (1996)**
    - **Tremors 3: Back to Perfection (2001)**
    - **Tremors: Shrieker Island (2020)**

3. Keep Spirits High

- Encourage positive energy with humorous commentary or cheering during dramatic moments.

22.8 End-of-Marathon Celebration
1. Group Photo

- Take a group photo to commemorate surviving the marathon. Use the photo booth setup or take a spontaneous snapshot.

2. Awards and Prizes

- Award prizes for categories like **"Most Attentive Viewer"**, **"Best Graboid Impression"**, or **"Most Bingo Wins."**

3. Final Toast

- Raise a glass of **Seismic Spiced Punch (Chapter 12)** or cocoa for a final toast to the Graboids and the *Tremors* franchise.

22.9 Example Schedule for a One-Day Marathon

Time	Activity
9:00 AM	Guests arrive, grab light snacks
9:30 AM	Movie 1: *Tremors (1990)*
11:15 AM	15-minute intermission (discussion)
11:30 AM	Movie 2: *Tremors 2: Aftershocks*
1:15 PM	45-minute lunch break (Desert Feast)
2:00 PM	Movie 3: *Tremors 3: Back to Perfection*
3:45 PM	15-minute intermission (Graboid Bingo)
4:00 PM	Movie 4: *Tremors 4: The Legend Begins*
6:00 PM	Dinner break (Graboid Guts Stew)
6:45 PM	Movie 5: *Tremors 5: Bloodlines*
8:30 PM	Dessert break (Tremors Cake)
8:45 PM	Movie 6: *Tremors: A Cold Day in Hell*
10:30 PM	Final Movie: *Tremors: Shrieker Island*

Time	Activity
12:15 AM	Closing toast and awards

Conclusion: Surviving the Marathon with Style

By planning breaks, incorporating fun activities, and providing plenty of food and drink, you'll ensure that your *Tremors* movie marathon is a thrilling success. With the right pacing, your guests will leave feeling entertained, satisfied, and fully immersed in the chaotic charm of Perfection, NV. Whether it's a one-day binge or a weekend-long adventure, your marathon will be a monstrous event to remember!

Chapter 23: Graboid Movie Trivia Challenge

Inject extra fun and friendly competition into your *Tremors* movie marathon with the **Graboid Movie Trivia Challenge**. This trivia game brings guests together to test their knowledge of the *Tremors* franchise, encouraging lively discussions and highlighting the series' quirks, characters, and monsters. Whether played between films or during breaks, the trivia challenge adds a dynamic element to your marathon and ensures everyone stays engaged.

23.1 The Concept: Competitive Fun with a Tremors Twist

The *Graboid Movie Trivia Challenge* is a structured quiz game where players answer questions about the *Tremors* movies, characters, creatures, and memorable moments.

- **Interactive**: Encourages group participation and friendly banter.
- **Educational**: Offers fun facts about the *Tremors* universe.
- **Customizable**: Suitable for fans of all knowledge levels, with questions ranging from easy to expert.

23.2 Setting Up the Game

1. Materials Needed

- **Trivia Questions**: Prepare a mix of multiple-choice, true/false, and open-ended questions (samples provided below).
- **Answer Sheets or Buzzers**: Use printed answer sheets, dry-erase boards, or small buzzers for players to indicate their answers.
- **Scoreboard**: Track individual or team scores on a whiteboard or large piece of paper.
- **Prizes**: Offer small, themed rewards for winners (see suggestions in Section 23.8).

2. Group Configuration

- **Individual Play**: Each guest competes on their own.
- **Team Play**: Divide guests into small teams to encourage collaboration. Teams can name themselves after *Tremors* themes (e.g., **Team Graboid**, **Team Perfection Survivors**, or **Team Burt's Arsenal**).

3. Timing

- Play a round of trivia during each intermission or dedicate a single longer break for the entire challenge.
- Each round can last 10–15 minutes, depending on the number of questions.

23.3 Trivia Categories

Divide your questions into categories to structure the game and keep it exciting. Here are a few examples:

1. Classic Quotes

- Identify famous lines from the movies or guess which character said them.

2. Graboid Biology

- Test knowledge about the creatures' lifecycle, abilities, and unique traits.

3. Perfection, NV

- Questions about the town's residents, landmarks, and history.

4. Weapons and Gear

- A category for Burt Gummer enthusiasts, focusing on his arsenal and survival tactics.

5. Behind-the-Scenes

- Trivia about the making of the movies, such as directors, filming locations, and special effects.

23.4 Sample Trivia Questions
Classic Quotes

1. **"Broke into the wrong goddamn rec room, didn't you?"**
    - Who said this iconic line?
    - **Answer**: Burt Gummer
2. **"We've got to do something! We've got to think!"**
    - Which character said this in *Tremors (1990)*?
    - **Answer**: Valentine "Val" McKee

Graboid Biology

1. What is the second stage of a Graboid's life cycle?
    - a) Dirt Dragon
    - b) Shrieker
    - c) Ass-Blaster
    - d) Alpha Graboid
    - **Answer**: b) Shrieker
2. True or False: Graboids have no eyes.
    - **Answer**: True

Perfection, NV

1. What is the name of the general store in Perfection?
    - **Answer**: Walter Chang's Market
2. How many residents lived in Perfection at the start of *Tremors (1990)*?
    - **Answer**: 14

Weapons and Gear

1. What caliber rifle does Burt Gummer famously use to kill a Graboid in *Tremors (1990)*?
    - a) .50 BMG
    - b) .375 H&H
    - c) .30-06 Springfield
    - d) .223 Remington
    - **Answer**: a) .50 BMG
2. In *Tremors 2: Aftershocks*, what improvised explosive does Earl use to kill Shriekers?

  - ◦ **Answer**: Remote-controlled car with dynamite

Behind-the-Scenes

1. Who directed the original *Tremors* film?
   - ◦ **Answer**: Ron Underwood
2. In which desert was *Tremors (1990)* primarily filmed?
   - ◦ **Answer**: Alabama Hills, Lone Pine, California

23.5 Bonus Round: Lightning Graboid

Introduce a bonus round at the end of each trivia session:

- Ask rapid-fire questions where players must shout their answers.
- Examples:
  - ◦ **"Name all three life stages of a Graboid!"**
  - ◦ **"What year was *Tremors* released?"**

23.6 Scoring System
Points

- **Easy Questions**: 1 point
- **Medium Questions**: 2 points
- **Hard Questions**: 3 points

Tie-Breaker

If there's a tie, ask a challenging, open-ended question to determine the winner. Example:

- **"Describe Burt Gummer's role in the evolution of Graboid hunting techniques."**

23.7 Hosting Tips
1. Encourage Team Spirit

- Use team names and cheers to foster excitement.
- Allow teams to discuss answers (within a time limit) for tougher questions.

2. Add Thematic Rewards

- Offer points for creative answers, even if they're incorrect, as long as they're entertaining or *Tremors*-relevant.

3. Include Visual Aids

- Display stills from the movies for visual questions (e.g., **"Name this character"** or **"Identify this weapon"**).

23.8 Prizes for Winners
Thematic Prizes

- Small toy Graboids or custom-made figurines
- *Tremors* posters or DVDs
- Survival gear props like mini flashlights or compasses

Fun Awards

- **"Graboid Guru"**: For the overall winner
- **"Burt's Apprentice"**: For the best weapons knowledge
- **"Perfection's Historian"**: For knowledge about the town

23.9 Alternate Formats
Interactive Trivia Board

- Create a physical or digital trivia board with categories and point values (like *Jeopardy*).

Mobile Trivia App

- Use quiz apps like Kahoot! to host a digital trivia game with guests answering on their phones.

Conclusion: Tremors Trivia for the Win
The *Graboid Movie Trivia Challenge* brings an exciting, competitive element to your *Tremors* marathon, highlighting the franchise's best moments and deepening everyone's appreciation for the

series. With engaging questions, lively discussions, and thematic prizes, the trivia challenge is sure to be a highlight of your *Tremors Wonderland*. Whether played between films or as a standalone event, this game guarantees laughs, learning, and a memorable time for all.

Chapter 24: DIY Tremors Viewing Tent

Transform your movie marathon space into an immersive *Tremors* hideout by building a **DIY Viewing Tent** or fort. Modeled after the survivalist spirit of the *Tremors* franchise, this indoor shelter provides a cozy, thematic space to "hide" from Graboids while watching the movies. Perfect for families, kids, or fans looking for a creative twist, the tent enhances the movie experience by evoking the tension and fun of escaping underground monsters.

24.1 The Concept: A Survivalist Hideout

In the world of *Tremors*, survival often means staying hidden and out of reach of Graboids. Your DIY viewing tent brings that spirit to life by creating a safe, cozy space that feels like a survivalist bunker or desert refuge. The tent should balance:

- **Comfort**: Soft pillows, blankets, and plenty of room for snacks.
- **Thematic Elements**: Decorations inspired by Perfection, NV, and the *Tremors* universe.
- **Interactivity**: Details like "Graboid warnings" and interactive props to keep guests engaged.

24.2 Materials and Tools
Core Structure

- Large bedsheets, blankets, or canvas fabric (neutral tones like beige, brown, or green work best).
- Furniture to act as a frame (e.g., chairs, couches, tables).
- Heavy-duty clips or clothespins to secure the fabric.
- String lights or LED strips for lighting.

Decorations

- Faux rocks (foam or crumpled paper painted gray or brown).
- Green craft paper or small fake plants for desert shrubs.
- Toy Graboids or licorice ropes to simulate monster tentacles.
- Signs like **"Graboid Warning Zone"** or **"Danger: Seismic Activity."**

Comfort Items

- Pillows and cushions for seating.
- Throw blankets for warmth.
- Small side tables or trays for snacks and drinks.

Optional Extras

- A small projector or tablet for screening movies inside the tent.
- A fan for airflow, especially in larger tents.

24.3 Building the Tent
Step 1: Choose a Location

- **Living Room**: A central spot near your main movie screen is ideal.
- **Cozy Corner**: For smaller setups, use a corner of the room to create a compact, intimate tent.

Step 2: Build the Frame

- Arrange furniture like chairs or couches to form the tent's structure.
- For a larger tent, use tall objects like bookshelves or clothing racks to elevate the roof.

Step 3: Drape the Fabric

- Spread sheets or blankets over the frame, securing them with clips or clothespins.
- Leave an opening for easy entry and exit, or create a "flap door" for added fun.

Step 4: Add Thematic Details

- Scatter faux rocks and plants around the tent's base to mimic a desert landscape.
- Hang **"Warning"** or **"Survival Zone"** signs on the outside.
- Drape licorice ropes or small toy Graboids from the edges to simulate Graboid attacks.

24.4 Lighting the Tent
Ambient Lighting

- Use string lights or LED strips to create a warm, inviting glow inside the tent.
- Drape the lights around the tent's interior edges for even illumination.

Thematic Effects

- Add flickering LED candles for a "campfire" vibe.
- Use colored LED lights (red or orange) to simulate a desert sunset or seismic activity.

24.5 Furnishing the Interior
Comfort Essentials

- Arrange soft pillows and cushions for comfortable seating.
- Use plush blankets for warmth and coziness.

Snack Station

- Include a small table or tray for themed snacks like **Graboid Popcorn Mix (Chapter 15)** or **Tentacle Breadsticks (Chapter 13).**
- Add cup holders or spill-proof trays for drinks like **Wormy Hot Chocolate (Chapter 10)** or **Seismic Spiced Punch (Chapter 12).**

Viewing Gear

- Set up a small projector or tablet to screen movies directly inside the tent for a unique viewing experience.
- Include headphones or speakers to ensure good sound quality.

24.6 Interactive Tent Features
1. Graboid Alarm

- Attach a small bell or motion-activated light to the tent's entrance to alert "survivors" of Graboid activity.

2. Escape Hatch

- Create a "hidden exit" by leaving one side of the tent slightly open and labeling it as an emergency escape route.

3. Thematic Props

- Include survival gear like flashlights, compasses, or toy weapons for added immersion.
- Add toy trucks or figurines inside the tent to simulate Perfection, NV, life.

24.7 Tent Themes for Different Audiences
For Families with Kids

- Add playful elements like coloring pages, Graboid plushies, or DIY craft kits for making mini Graboids.

For Hardcore Fans

- Include detailed decorations like maps of Perfection, NV, or replicas of Burt Gummer's survivalist gear.

For Couples

- Create a romantic desert hideaway with soft lighting, cozy blankets, and themed snacks for two.

24.8 Hosting Tips
1. Encourage Participation

- Let guests help decorate the tent or add their own personal touches.

2. Rotate Use

- If space is limited, allow guests to take turns enjoying the tent during the marathon.

3. Photo Opportunities

- Use the tent as a backdrop for themed photos. Provide props like cowboy hats, toy Graboids, or survival gear.

24.9 Maintenance and Cleanup
During the Marathon

- Keep a small trash bag or bin inside the tent for easy cleanup of snack wrappers.
- Provide coasters or spill-proof cups for drinks.

After the Event

- Carefully dismantle the tent, folding and storing fabric and decorations for future use.
- Vacuum the area to remove crumbs or debris.

Conclusion: A Shelter from the Graboids

The **DIY Tremors Viewing Tent** is more than just a fun decoration—it's an interactive, immersive element that brings the *Tremors* marathon to life. By combining comfort, creativity, and thematic details, the tent becomes a centerpiece of your event, offering a cozy hideout for guests to enjoy. Whether you're building a large group tent or a small corner refuge, this project will leave a lasting impression and elevate your *Tremors Wonderland* experience.

Chapter 25: The Ultimate Tremors Movie Awards

Cap off your *Tremors* marathon with a fun and festive **Tremors Movie Awards Ceremony**, celebrating the best moments, characters, and monsters from the series. This chapter provides a detailed guide to hosting an awards show, complete with printable templates for categories, trophies, and nomination cards. By letting your guests vote for their favorites, you'll turn the end of your marathon into a collaborative and entertaining finale.

25.1 The Concept: A Celebration of Tremors Excellence

The *Tremors* Movie Awards lets fans recognize the most iconic, hilarious, and jaw-dropping moments from the series. Guests vote on categories like "Best Graboid Kill," "Favorite Character," and "Most Ridiculous Weapon," turning the marathon into an interactive event that highlights what makes *Tremors* so beloved.

25.2 Planning the Awards Ceremony

1. Timing

- Host the awards ceremony immediately after the final movie to keep the excitement alive.
- Allocate 30–45 minutes for the event, depending on the number of categories.

2. Materials Needed

- **Printable Ballots**: Provide pre-made ballots with all the award categories.
- **Award Certificates or Trophies**: Create custom certificates or purchase small trophies for winners.
- **Decorations**: Set up a mini stage or podium with a microphone for announcements.
- **Themed Envelopes**: Use gold or desert-inspired envelopes to reveal the winners.

3. Voting Process

- Before the ceremony, distribute ballots to guests and let them vote during intermissions or after the final movie.
- Collect ballots and tally the votes while showing the last film.

25.3 Suggested Award Categories
Monster Moments

1. **Best Graboid Appearance**
   - Awarded to the most dramatic or memorable Graboid reveal.
2. **Best Monster Evolution**
   - Nominees: Shriekers, Ass-Blasters, Arctic Graboids, etc.
3. **Most Shocking Graboid Kill**
   - Recognizes the most surprising or inventive way a Graboid was defeated.

Characters

1. **Best Character in the Series**
   - Who stood out across all the movies?
2. **Best One-Liner or Quote**
   - Example: Burt Gummer's **"I am completely out of ammo!"**
3. **Best Sidekick**
   - Nominees: Earl, Travis, or other supporting heroes.

Scenes and Action

1. **Best Explosion**
   - Celebrate the biggest, loudest, and most dramatic explosion.
2. **Most Creative Weapon**
   - Highlight Burt Gummer's unique arsenal or improvised tools.
3. **Best Team Plan Gone Wrong**
   - Awarded to the most hilariously disastrous survival strategy.

Special Awards

1. **The Graboid Lifetime Achievement Award**
   - Honors the most iconic or beloved monster of the series.
2. **Most Ridiculous Moment**
   - From Ass-Blasters to over-the-top stunts, this award goes to the most absurd scene.
3. **Best Location in the Series**
   - Nominees: Perfection, NV; South Africa (*Tremors 5*); the Arctic (*Tremors: A Cold Day in Hell*), etc.

25.4 Printable Ballot Template

Instructions: Print the ballot below and distribute to your guests for voting.

The Ultimate Tremors Movie Awards Ballot

1. **Best Graboid Appearance:** _______________________________
2. **Best Monster Evolution:** _______________________________
3. **Most Shocking Graboid Kill:** _______________________________
4. **Best Character in the Series:** _______________________
5. **Best One-Liner or Quote:** _______________________
6. **Best Sidekick:** _______________________________
7. **Best Explosion:** _______________________________
8. **Most Creative Weapon:** _______________________
9. **Best Team Plan Gone Wrong:** _______________________
10. **Graboid Lifetime Achievement Award:** _______________
11. **Most Ridiculous Moment:** _______________________
12. **Best Location in the Series:** _______________

25.5 Hosting the Awards Ceremony

1. Create a Festive Atmosphere

- Use string lights, gold decorations, and a backdrop featuring Graboids or desert imagery to set the stage.
- Provide a small microphone or prop for the "host" to use when announcing winners.

2. Announce Nominees

- For each category, list the nominees before revealing the winner. Example:
  - **Best Graboid Appearance**:
    - The Graboid bursting through the ground in *Tremors (1990)*.
    - The first Shrieker attack in *Tremors 2: Aftershocks*.
    - The Arctic Graboid's reveal in *Tremors: A Cold Day in Hell*.

3. Reveal the Winners

- Open a themed envelope or unfold a certificate for each winner.
- Add dramatic pauses and playful commentary to keep the audience engaged.

4. Distribute Prizes

- Award winners with small trophies, medals, or fun-themed items like toy Graboids, posters, or survival gear.

25.6 Example Printable Certificate
The Ultimate Tremors Movie Awards
This Certificate is Awarded To:
[Winner's Name]
For:
[Category Name]
Signed:
The Perfection Movie Marathon Host
Date: _________________

25.7 Prizes for Winners
Thematic Prizes

- Graboid action figures or plush toys.
- Posters or DVDs of *Tremors*.
- Custom Graboid-themed mugs or tumblers.
- Survival-themed prizes like mini flashlights or multitools.

Funny Awards

- **"Burt's Arsenal Badge"**: For Best Weapon-related categories.
- **"Graboid's Nemesis Trophy"**: For Best Monster Kill.
- **"Honorary Perfection Resident Certificate"**: For standout guests or MVP participants.

25.8 Closing the Event
Final Toast

- Wrap up the ceremony with a toast to the *Tremors* franchise, using **Seismic Spiced Punch (Chapter 12)** or cocoa.

Group Photo

- Take a celebratory photo with all the winners and their prizes to commemorate the night.

Thank You Speech

- Thank your guests for joining the marathon and making the awards ceremony a success.

Conclusion: A Monster Celebration to Remember
The **Ultimate Tremors Movie Awards** is the perfect way to celebrate the franchise while engaging your guests in friendly competition. By recognizing the best moments, characters, and scenes,

you'll end your *Tremors Wonderland* marathon with laughter, excitement, and a deeper appreciation for the series. Whether you keep it lighthearted or go all out with dramatic flair, this awards ceremony will be a highlight of the event, leaving your guests with fond memories and a renewed love for the Graboids.

Appendix A: Printable Templates and Guides

This appendix contains a variety of ready-to-use printable templates and guides to make your *Tremors Wonderland* event both creative and organized. From Bingo cards to craft outlines and movie awards sheets, these resources will enhance the experience for your guests, helping you create a cohesive and engaging event.

A.1 Tremors Bingo Cards
How to Use

- Print out one Bingo card for each guest.
- Provide markers (stickers, pens, or candies) to mark squares during the movie.
- Use the Bingo rules outlined in **Chapter 20** to guide gameplay.

Sample Bingo Card (5x5 Grid)

Burt Gummer Quote	Explosion Happens	Graboid Seen	Climbs a Rock	Hero Sacrifice
Truck Breaks Down	Map of Perfection Seen	Someone Screams	Shrieker Detected	Improvised Weapon
Plan Fails	FREE SPACE	Burt Eats Snack	Tentacle Grabs Someone	Graboid Tunnel Scene
"We Gotta Get Out!"	Melvin's Sarcastic Line	Cactus Seen	Heat Vision Used	Danger Sign Ignored

A.2 Tremors Gift Tags
How to Use

- Print the gift tags on cardstock or heavy paper.
- Cut out the tags along the dotted lines and attach them to gifts using string or ribbon.

Sample Gift Tag Designs

1. **"From the Graboids: Handle with Care!"**
2. **"Survive the Holidays, Perfection Style!"**
3. **"Burt Approved: A Survivalist's Gift!"**
4. **"Merry Tremors and a Happy New Graboid!"**

A.3 Craft Outlines
DIY Graboid Ornament Template
Materials Needed:

- Cardstock or thin cardboard for the base.
- Paint or markers to decorate.
- String or hooks for hanging.

Template Instructions:

1. Print the Graboid ornament outline onto sturdy paper.
2. Cut along the solid lines to create the base shape.
3. Decorate the ornament with paints or markers to resemble a Graboid, adding details like eyes and tentacles.
4. Punch a hole at the top and thread string through for hanging.

Tentacle Breadstick Mold Guide
Materials Needed:

- Printable template for shaping dough.
- Wax paper or parchment paper for baking.

Template Instructions:

1. Print the tentacle outline and place it under wax paper.
2. Shape breadstick dough along the outline, adding twists and indentations for texture.

3. Bake according to the recipe in **Chapter 13**.

A.4 Movie Awards Sheets
Award Certificate Template
Template Layout:

- Title: **The Ultimate Tremors Movie Awards**
- Awardee: **[Winner's Name]**
- Category: **[Category Name]**
- Signature: **[Host's Name]**
- Date: **[Event Date]**

How to Use:

1. Print the template onto heavyweight paper.
2. Fill in the blanks with the winner's name and category.
3. Present certificates during the awards ceremony as described in **Chapter 25**.

Ballot Template

Category	Nominee Options
Best Graboid Appearance	1. *Tremors (1990)* Graboids bursting through the ground. 2. Shrieker reveal in *Tremors 2*.
Most Shocking Graboid Kill	1. Explosive truck trap in *Tremors (1990)*. 2. Remote car dynamite in *Tremors 2*.
Best Character in the Series	1. Burt Gummer. 2. Val McKee. 3. Earl Bassett.

A.5 Tent Construction Guide
Tent Blueprint
Materials Checklist:

- 4 sturdy chairs or two couches for structure.
- 3–4 large sheets or blankets for covering.
- Clothespins or heavy-duty clips for securing.

Step-by-Step Instructions:

1. Arrange chairs in a rectangular formation with two on each side, leaving an opening for the tent entrance.
2. Drape the sheets over the chairs, making sure the fabric overlaps for full coverage.
3. Secure the sheets to the chair backs with clips.
4. Decorate the interior with pillows, string lights, and Graboid props as described in **Chapter 24**.

A.6 Additional Printable Decorations
Perfection, NV Sign

- **Text**: "Welcome to Perfection, NV: Population 14 (Watch for Graboids!)"
- Print on cardstock and mount on a stand or wall.

Graboid Warning Signs

- **Text Options**:
  1. "Danger: Seismic Activity Ahead!"
  2. "Stay Off the Ground: Graboids Active!"
  3. "Warning: Graboid Nest Nearby!"

Character Quotes Posters

- Print memorable quotes from the series, such as:
  - "Broke into the wrong goddamn rec room, didn't you?" – Burt Gummer
  - "It's not gonna stop, Earl!" – Valentine McKee

How to Access and Customize Templates

1. Download templates from your preferred design software or print-ready websites.
2. Use editable PDF files for customized text and designs.
3. Print on high-quality paper or cardstock for durability.

Conclusion: Ready-to-Use Resources for Tremors Wonderland
This appendix provides all the tools you need to enhance your *Tremors Wonderland* event. From interactive Bingo cards to themed gift tags and craft outlines, these printable templates make it easy to bring your creative vision to life. Customize them to match your theme, print them for your guests, and let the *Tremors*-themed fun take center stage!

Appendix B: Shopping and Resource List

This appendix provides a comprehensive guide to gathering everything you need for your *Tremors Wonderland* event. From craft supplies and snacks to decorations and streaming resources, this shopping list ensures you'll be well-prepared to create a seamless and immersive experience for your guests.

B.1 Materials for Crafts

For Graboid Garlands and Ornaments (Chapter 1)

- **Cardstock or Thin Cardboard**: For crafting Graboid shapes.
- **Acrylic Paints or Markers**: In shades of brown, black, red, and gray.
- **String or Ribbon**: To hang ornaments and garlands.
- **Glue or Hot Glue Gun**: For assembling pieces.
- **Scissors or Craft Knife**: For cutting shapes.
- **Glitter or Metallic Paint**: Optional, for festive touches.

For DIY Graboid Snow Globes (Chapter 6)

- **Clear Plastic or Glass Jars**: Mason jars work well.
- **Miniature Figurines**: Graboids, cacti, or desert-themed miniatures.
- **Glycerin**: To thicken the water for snow effects.
- **Distilled Water**: For filling the globes.
- **Glitter or Faux Snowflakes**: For the "snow" effect.
- **Strong Adhesive**: To secure figurines to jar lids.

For Tremors Viewing Tent (Chapter 24)

- **Large Bedsheets or Blankets**: Preferably in neutral tones (beige, brown, or green).
- **Clips or Clothespins**: To secure fabric to furniture.
- **String Lights or Battery-Operated LED Lights**: For interior ambiance.
- **Faux Rocks and Plants**: Foam rocks, painted paper, or small plastic plants for desert decorations.

B.2 Recommended Snacks and Drinks
Savory Snacks

- **Popcorn**: For **Graboid Popcorn Mix (Chapter 15)**.
    - Add-ons: Mini pretzels, cheese powder, gummy worms, and caramel drizzle.
- **Breadstick Dough**: For **Tentacle Breadsticks (Chapter 13)**.
    - Buy pre-made dough or ingredients for homemade dough (flour, yeast, olive oil, salt).

Main Course Ingredients

- **Roast Beef or Chicken**: For **Graboid Guts Stew (Chapter 9)** or **Desert Feast (Chapter 14)**.
- **Vegetables**: Carrots, celery, and potatoes for hearty sides.

Sweet Treats

- **Marshmallows and Licorice**: For **Wormy Hot Chocolate Bar (Chapter 10)**.
- **Cupcake Mix and Icing**: For **Graboids in the Snow Cupcakes (Chapter 11)**.
    - Additional: Red licorice ropes and gummy worms for decoration.

Drinks

- **Cider, Juice, or Soda**: For **Seismic Spiced Punch (Chapter 12)**.
- **Hot Cocoa Powder and Milk**: For **Wormy Hot Chocolate Bar (Chapter 10)**.

B.3 Decorations
Thematic Items

- **Posters or Artwork**: *Tremors* movie posters or custom-printed designs.
- **Faux Rocks and Cacti**: Buy from craft stores or online. Foam or paper mache options are lightweight and easy to move.
- **Toy Graboids or Tentacles**: Look for small figurines, licorice ropes, or bendable rubber for realistic effects.

Lighting and Atmosphere

- **String Lights**: Warm or desert-themed colors.
- **LED Candles**: For a "campfire" vibe inside tents or around tables.
- **Colored Bulbs**: Red or orange bulbs to simulate desert sunsets or seismic activity.

Props and Accessories

- **Survival Gear Props**: Plastic flashlights, toy compasses, and fake weapons to match the *Tremors* survivalist theme.
- **Graboid Warning Signs**: Craft your own or purchase pre-made party signs.

B.4 Streaming and Purchasing Tremors Movies
Streaming Platforms

- **Amazon Prime Video**: Rent or buy all seven *Tremors* movies in HD.
- **Peacock**: Some *Tremors* movies may be available with a subscription.
- **Apple TV/iTunes**: Offers individual movie rentals or purchases.
- **Google Play Movies**: Digital rentals and purchases of *Tremors* films.
- **YouTube Movies**: Pay-per-view rentals or purchases.
- **Netflix**: Occasionally includes certain *Tremors* titles in its catalog.

Physical Media

- **DVD/Blu-ray Collections**:
  - Look for *Tremors: The Complete Collection*, which includes all seven movies.
  - Available on Amazon, Walmart, or Best Buy.

Behind-the-Scenes Content

- Check YouTube or special edition DVDs for bonus features like interviews, making-of documentaries, and deleted scenes.

B.5 Where to Buy Everything
Craft Supplies

- **Michaels**: Crafting tools, paints, and faux plants.
- **Hobby Lobby**: Decorations and crafting supplies, including foam rocks.
- **Joann Fabrics**: Fabrics for tents and garlands.
- **Amazon**: Bulk orders of crafting materials, lights, and small decorations.

Snacks and Ingredients

- **Grocery Stores**: Local supermarkets for popcorn, breadstick dough, and ingredients for stews and desserts.
- **Bulk Retailers**: Costco or Sam's Club for large quantities of snacks and drinks.
- **Online Specialty Stores**: Websites like Nuts.com for unique toppings and candies.

Decorations and Props

- **Party City**: Themed party decorations like banners and signs.
- **Etsy**: Custom-made Graboid figures, signs, and themed crafts.
- **eBay**: Collectibles and rare *Tremors* memorabilia.

Movie Resources

- **Amazon**: Best for physical and digital movie purchases.
- **Vudu**: An alternative for digital rentals.

Conclusion: Comprehensive Prep for a Perfect Event

With this detailed shopping and resource list, you'll have everything you need to bring your *Tremors Wonderland* to life. From crafts and snacks to streaming the full movie series, this guide ensures your event is well-organized, immersive, and unforgettable. Whether you're hosting a small gathering or a large marathon, these resources will help you create a seamless experience filled with fun, creativity, and monster-sized memories.

Message from the Author:

I hope you enjoyed this book, I love astrology and knew there was not a book such as this out on the shelf. I love metaphysical items as well. Please check out my other books:

-Life of Government Benefits

-My life of Hell

-My life with Hydrocephalus

-Red Sky

-World Domination:Woman's rule

-World Domination:Woman's Rule 2: The War

-Life and Banishment of Apophis: book 1

-The Kidney Friendly Diet

-The Ultimate Hemp Cookbook

-Creating a Dispensary(legally)

-Cleanliness throughout life: the importance of showering from childhood to adulthood.

-Strong Roots: The Risks of Overcoddling children

-Hemp Horoscopes: Cosmic Insights and Earthly Healing

- Celestial Hemp Navigating the Zodiac: Through the Green Cosmos

-Astrological Hemp: Aligning The Stars with Earth's Ancient Herb

-The Astrological Guide to Hemp: Stars, Signs, and Sacred Leaves

-Green Growth: Innovative Marketing Strategies for your Hemp Products and Dispensary

-Cosmic Cannabis

-Astrological Munchies

-Henry The Hemp

-Zodiacal Roots: The Astrological Soul Of Hemp

- **Green Constellations: Intersection of Hemp and Zodiac**

-Hemp in The Houses: An astrological Adventure Through The Cannabis Galaxy

-Galactic Ganja Guide

Heavenly Hemp

Zodiac Leaves

Doctor Who Astrology

Cannastrology

Stellar Satvias and Cosmic Indicas

Celestial Cannabis: A Zodiac Journey

AstroHerbology: The Sky and The Soil: Volume 1

AstroHerbology:Celestial Cannabis:Volume 2

Cosmic Cannabis Cultivation

The Starry Guide to Herbal Harmony: Volume 1

The Starry Guide to Herbal Harmony: Cannabis Universe: Volume 2

Yugioh Astrology: Astrological Guide to Deck, Duels and more

Nightmare Mansion: Echoes of The Abyss

Nightmare Mansion 2: Legacy of Shadows

Nightmare Mansion 3: Shadows of the Forgotten

Nightmare Mansion 4: Echoes of the Damned

The Life and Banishment of Apophis: Book 2

Nightmare Mansion: Halls of Despair

<u>Healing with Herb: Cannabis and Hydrocephalus</u>

<u>Planetary Pot: Aligning with Astrological Herbs: Volume 1</u>

Fast Track to Freedom: 30 Days to Financial Independence Using AI, Assets, and Agile Hustles

<u>Cosmic Hemp Pathways</u>

How to Become Financially Free in 30 Days: 10,000 Paths to Prosperity

Zodiacal Herbage: Astrological Insights: Volume 1

Nightmare Mansion: Whispers in the Walls

The Daleks Invade Atlantis

Henry the hemp and Hydrocephalus

10X The Kidney Friendly Diet

Cannabis Universe: Adult coloring book

Hemp Astrology: The Healing Power of the Stars

Zodiacal Herbage: Astrological Insights: Cannabis Universe: Volume 2

<u>Planetary Pot: Aligning with Astrological Herbs: Cannabis Universes: Volume 2</u>

Doctor Who Meets the Replicators and SG-1: The Ultimate Battle for Survival

Nightmare Mansion: Curse of the Blood Moon

<u>The Celestial Stoner: A Guide to the Zodiac</u>

Cosmic Pleasures: Sex Toy Astrology for Every Sign

Hydrocephalus Astrology: Navigating the Stars and Healing Waters

Lapis and the Mischievous Chocolate Bar

Celestial Positions: Sexual Astrology for Every Sign

Apophis's Shadow Work Journal: : A Journey of Self-Discovery and Healing

Kinky Cosmos: Sexual Kink Astrology for Every Sign

Digital Cosmos: The Astrological Digimon Compendium

Stellar Seeds: The Cosmic Guide to Growing with Astrology

Apophis's Daily Gratitude Journal

Cat Astrology: Feline Mysteries of the Cosmos

The Cosmic Kama Sutra: An Astrological Guide to Sexual Positions

Unleash Your Potential: A Guided Journal Powered by AI Insights

Whispers of the Enchanted Grove

Cosmic Pleasures: An Astrological Guide to Sexual Kinks

369, 12 Manifestation Journal

Whisper of the nocturne journal(blank journal for writing or drawing)

The Boogey Book

Locked In Reflection: A Chastity Journey Through Locktober

Generating Wealth Quickly:

How to Generate $100,000 in 24 Hours

Star Magic: Harness the Power of the Universe

The Flatulence Chronicles: A Fart Journal for Self-Discovery

The Doctor and The Death Moth

Seize the Day: A Personal Seizure Tracking Journal

The Ultimate Boogeyman Safari: A Journey into the Boogie World and Beyond

Whispers of Samhain: 1,000 Spells of Love, Luck, and Lunar Magic: Samhain Spell Book

Apophis's guides:

Witch's Spellbook Crafting Guide for Halloween

<u>Frost & Flame: The Enchanted Yule Grimoire of 1000 Winter Spells</u>

<u>The Ultimate Boogey Goo Guide & Spooky Activities for Halloween Fun</u>

Harmony of the Scales: A Libra's Spellcraft for Balance and Beauty

The Enchanted Advent: 36 Days of Christmas Wonders

Nightmare Mansion: The Labyrinth of Screams

Harvest of Enchantment: 1,000 Spells of Gratitude, Love, and Fortune for Thanksgiving

The Boogey Chronicles: A Journal of Nightly Encounters and Shadowy Secrets

The 12 Days of Financial Freedom: A Step-by-Step Christmas Countdown to Transform Your Finances

Sigil of the Eternal Spiral Blank Journal

A Christmas Feast: Timeless Recipes for Every Meal

Holiday Stress-Free Solutions: A Survival Guide to Thriving During the Festive Season

Yu-Gi-Oh! Holiday Gifting Mastery: The Ultimate Guide for Fans and Newcomers Alike

Holiday Harmony: A Hydrocephalus Survival Guide for the Festive Season

Celestial Craft: The Witch's Almanac for 2025 – A Cosmic Guide to Manifestations, Moons, and Mystical Events

Doctor Who: The Toymaker's Winter Wonderland

Tulsa King Unveiled: A Thrilling Guide to Stallone's Mafia Masterpiece

Pendulum Craft: A Complete Guide to Crafting and Using Personalized Divination Tools

Nightmare Mansion: Santa's Eternal Eve

Starlight Noel: A Cosmic Journey through Christmas Mysteries

The Dark Architect: Unlocking the Blueprint of Existence

Surviving the Embrace: The Ultimate Guide to Encounters with The Hugging Molly

The Enchanted Codex: Secrets of the Craft for Witches, Wiccans, and Pagans

Harvest of Gratitude: A Complete Thanksgiving Guide

Yuletide Essentials: A Complete Guide to an Authentic and Magical Christmas
Celestial Smokes: A Cosmic Guide to Cigars and Astrology
Living in Balance: A Comprehensive Survival Guide to Thriving with Diabetes Insipidus
Cosmic Symbiosis: The Venom Zodiac Chronicles
The Cursed Paw of Ambition
Cosmic Symbiosis: The Astrological Venom Journal
Celestial Wonders Unfold: A Stargazer's Guide to the Cosmos (2024-2029)
The Ultimate Black Friday Prepper's Guide: Mastering Shopping Strategies and Savings
Cosmic Sales: The Astrological Guide to Black Friday Shopping
Legends of the Corn Mother and Other Harvest Myths
Whispers of the Harvest: The Corn Mother's Journal
The Evergreen Spellbook
The Doctor Meets the Boogeyman
The White Witch of Rose Hall's SpellBook
The Gingerbread Golem's Shadow: A Study in Sweet Darkness
The Gingerbread Golem Codex: An Academic Exploration of Sweet Myths
The Gingerbread Golem Grimoire: Sweet Magicks and Spells for the Festive Witch
The Curse of the Gingerbread Golem
10-minute Christmas Crafts for kids
<u>Christmas Crisis Solutions: The Ultimate Last-Minute Survival Guide</u>
Gingerbread Golem Recipes: Holiday Treats with a Magical Twist
The Infinite Key: Unlocking Mystical Secrets of the Ages
Enchanted Yule: A Wiccan and Pagan Guide to a Magical and Memorable Season
Dinosaurs of Power: Unlocking Ancient Magick
Astro-Dinos: The Cosmic Guide to Prehistoric Wisdom
Gallifrey's Yule Logs: A Festive Doctor Who Cookbook
The Dino Grimoire: Secrets of Prehistoric Magick
The Gift They Never Knew They Needed
The Gingerbread Golem's Culinary Alchemy: Enchanting Recipes for a Sweetly Dark Feast
A Time Lord Christmas: Holiday Adventures with the Doctor
Krampusproofing Your Home: Defensive Strategies for Yule
Silent Frights: A Collection of Christmas Creepypastas to Chill Your Bones
Santa Raptor's Jolly Carnage: A Dino-Claus Christmas Tale
Prehistoric Palettes: A Dino Wicca Coloring Journey
The Christmas Wishkeeper Chronicles
The Starlight Sleigh: A Holiday Journey
Elf Secrets: The True Magic of the North Pole
Candy Cane Conjurations
Cooking with Kids: Recipes Under 20 Minutes
Doctor Who: The TARDIS Confiscation
The Anxiety First Aid Kit: Quick Tools to Calm Your Mind

Frosty Whispers: A Winter's Tale
The Infinite Key: Unlocking the Secrets to Prosperity, Resilience, and Purpose
The Grasping Void: Why You'll Regret This Purchase
Astrology for Busy Bees: Star Signs Simplified
The Instant Focus Formula: Cut Through the Noise
The Secret Language of Colors: Unlocking the Emotional Codes
Sacred Fossil Chronicles: Blank Journal
The Christmas Cottage Miracle
Feeding Frenzy: Graboid-Inspired Recipes
Manifest in Minutes: The Quick Law of Attraction Guide
The Symbiote Chronicles: Doctor Who's Venomous Journey
Think Tiny, Grow Big: The Minimalist Mindset
The Energy Key: Unlocking Limitless Motivation
New Year, New Magic: Manifesting Your Best Year Yet
Unstoppable You: Mastering Confidence in Minutes
Infinite Energy: The Secret to Never Feeling Drained
Lightning Focus: Mastering the Art of Productivity in a Distracted World
Saturnalia Manifestation Magick: A Guide to Unlocking Abundance During the Solstice

If you want solar for your home go here: https://www.harborsolar.live/apophisenterprises/

Get Some Tarot cards: https://www.makeplayingcards.com/sell/apophis-occult-shop

Get some shirts: https://www.bonfire.com/store/apophis-shirt-emporium/

Instagrams:
@apophis_enterprises,
@apophisbookemporium,
@apophisscardshop
Twitter: @apophisenterpr1
Tiktok:@apophisenterprise
Youtube: @sg1fan23477, @FiresideRetreatKingdom
Hive: @sg1fan23477
CheeLee: @SG1fan23477

Podcast: Apophis Chat Zone: https://open.spotify.com/show/5zXbr-CLEV2xzCp8ybrfHsk?si=fb4d4fdbdce44dec

Newsletter: https://apophiss-newsletter-27c897.beehiiv.com/

If you want to support me or see posts of other projects that I have come over to: **buymeacof-fee.com/mpetchinskg**
I post there daily several times a day

Get your Dinowicca or Christmas themed digital products, especially Santa Raptor songs and other musics. Here: **https://sg1fan23477.gumroad.com**

Apophis Yuletide Digital has not only digital Christmas items, but it will have all things with Dinowicca as well as other Digital products.

9 798348 177225